LINDA GOODMAN

AQUARIUS

*Hope that this answers
a few questions - I think
it will answer woman.

Much love
Pamela*

Also by Linda Goodman in Pan Books

Linda Goodman's Love Signs

Linda Goodman's Sun Signs
(one volume)

Linda Goodman's Star Signs

LINDA GOODMAN'S SUN SIGNS

AQUARIUS
21 January to 19 February

Pan Books

London, Sydney and Auckland

First published in Great Britain 1970 by
George G. Harrap & Co Ltd
as part of a volume containing all twelve Sun signs
This edition published 1989 by Pan Books Ltd,
Cavaye Place, London SW10 9PG

10 9 8 7 6 5 4 3 2 1

© Linda Goodman 1968, 1989

ISBN 0 330 31010 0

Photoypeset by Input Typesetting Ltd, London
Printed and bound in Great Britain by
Richard Clay Ltd., Bungay, Suffolk

This book is sold subject to the condition that it shall not,
by way of trade or otherwise, be lent, re-sold,
hired out or otherwise circulated without the publisher's prior
consent in any form of binding or cover other than that
in which it is published and without a similar condition including
this condition being imposed on the subsequent purchaser.

For Mike Todd
the Gemini
who really knew the people he knew
and for Melissa Anne
the Pisces
to keep a promise . . .
Thus grew the tale of Wonderland:
Thus slowly, one by one,
Its quaint events were hammered out –
And now the tale is done . . .

Acknowledgement

I would like to express my grateful thanks for the help and advice given me by my friend and teacher, astrologer Lloyd Cope, a Virgo. Without his encouragement and faith, these books might have remained just another Aries dream.

The verses used throughout the text have been taken from the works of Lewis Carroll.

The term 'Sun sign' means that, if you are, for example, a Gemini, the Sun was in the zone of the zodiac called Gemini when you were born, approximately between 21 May and 21 June, inclusive. You'll find that the dates covering the Sun sign periods are slightly different, depending on which astrology book you read. Most astrologers don't wish to confuse the layman with the information that the Sun changes signs in the morning, afternoon or evening of a particular day. It's all very nice and neat and easy to pretend each new sign begins precisely at midnight. But it doesn't. For example, except for leap year variations, the Sun, for the last several decades as well as at the present, both leaves Aries and enters Taurus sometime on 20 April. It's important to know that 20 April contains both signs. Otherwise, you might go around all your life thinking you're a Taurus when you're really an Aries. Remember that if you were born on the *first* or the *last* day of any of the Sun sign periods, you'll have to know the exact time and the longitude and latitude of your birth to judge whether or not the Sun had changed signs by that hour.

Contents

Foreword

How to understand Sun signs

A tale begun in other days,
When summer suns were glowing –
A simple chime, that served to time
The rhythm of our rowing –

Some day, you will doubtless want the complete details
of your personal natal chart. Meanwhile, you can be sure
that studying your Sun sign is an important first step.
However, studying your Sun sign shouldn't be confused
with studying the predictions based on your Sun sign
alone in magazines and newspapers. They may hit you
with impressive accuracy more often than they miss, but
they're far from being infallible. Only a natal chart calculated for the exact hour and minute of your birth can be
completely dependable in such a specialized area.

On the other hand, don't believe the common accu-
sation that these predictions are 'just a bunch of general
phrases that can be scrambled around to fit anybody.'
That's equally untrue. The predictions (indications would
be a better word) apply as they are printed, to the Taurus
or Pisces or Virgo person individually. They don't apply
helter-skelter to any of the twelve Sun signs. They are
written by competent professionals and based on mathematical calculations of the aspects formed between your
natal Sun and the planets moving overhead, and they give
you a fair degree of accuracy, as far as they go. The fact
that they're not based on the *exact degree* of your natal

Sun, nor on the additional aspects from the other eight planets in your natal chart, plus your natal Moon, is what creates the flaw. Still, they can be interesting and helpful, if allowances are made for the discrepancies.

The Sun is the most powerful of all the stellar bodies. It colours the personality so strongly that an amazingly accurate picture can be given of the individual who was born when it was exercising its power through the known and predictable influences of a certain astrological sign. These electromagnetic vibrations (for want of a better term in the present stage of research) will continue to stamp that person with the characteristics of his Sun sign as he goes through life. The Sun isn't the only factor in analysing human behaviour and traits, but it's easily the most important single consideration.

Some astrologers feel that a book about Sun signs is a generalization comparable to lumping together all the Polish, Irish, Chinese, Negro, Italian and Jewish people – or like lumping all butchers, bakers, candlestick makers, merchants or Indian chiefs. Though I respect their feelings, I can't agree with them. True, Sun signs can be misleading if they're used with the wrong attitude. But in the absence of a natal chart, they're far ahead of any other known quick, reliable method of analysing people and learning to understand human nature.

An individual's Sun sign will be approximately eighty per cent accurate, sometimes up to ninety per cent. Isn't that far better than zero knowledge? That extra ten or twenty per cent is, of course, most important and must be considered. But if you know a person's Sun sign, you're substantially better informed than those who know nothing about him at all. There are no pitfalls in applying Sun sign knowledge when it's done with discretion. Just plant an imaginary policeman in your mind to keep warning you that you might be off by that ten or twenty per cent, and you can use them with confidence.

What is a Sun sign? A particular zone of the zodiac – Aries, Taurus, Gemini, etc. – in which the Sun was located at the moment you drew your first breath, an exact position taken from a set of tables called an ephemeris, calculated by astronomers. As printed out in the note to the reader that precedes the Table of Contents, if you were born on the *first* or the *last* day of any Sun sign period, you'll have to know your exact birth time and the longitude and latitude of your birth place to judge whether or not the sun had changed signs by that hour. In other words, the dates which begin and end the Sun sign periods in this or any astrology book are approximate, and this is most important to remember. These two days are called the cusps, and don't let them confuse you. Some astrologers even give them a longer period. But either way there's been entirely too much stress laid on them for the layman. No matter what you've heard, if the Sun was in Aquarius when you were born, it was in Aquarius, however near it may be to the cusp, and that's that. The influences which may be impressed on your personality from the sign preceding or following Aquarius will never blot out your Aquarian characteristics enough to turn you into a Capricorn or a Pisces. Nothing can dim the brilliance of the Sun, while it's actually in a sign, and the variations you get from being born on a cusp are never strong enough to substantially alter your basic Sun sign personality. The important thing is to establish through your birth hour that you were definitely born within the cusps. Make a small allowance for them, and then forget it.

What is a natal chart? You can think of it as a photograph of the exact position of all the planets in the sky at the moment of your birth, formed by precise mathematical calculation. In addition to the Sun and Moon (the two luminaries), there are eight planets, all of which influence your life, according to the signs they were in when you were born, their distance from each other by degrees (aspects) and their exact location.

If you were born on 9 February, you're an Aquarian, of course, because the Sun was in Aquarius, and about eight out of every ten Aquarian traits will show in your character. However, the Moon, ruling your emotions, might have been in Aries, colouring your emotional attitudes with Arian qualities. Mercury, ruling the mind, could have been in Scorpio, so your mental processes would often be Scorpion in nature. Mars, ruling your speech and movements, among other things, could have been in Taurus, so you would speak rather slowly, like a Taurean. Venus might have been in Capricorn, giving you an essentially Capricorn attitude in love, artistic and creative matters – and so on with the other planets. Yet, none of these placements will totally erase the basic qualities of your Aquarian Sun. They simply refine the details of your complex personality.

There are other factors to consider if you're to be one hundred per cent correctly analysed. For one thing, the aspects formed between the planets and the luminaries at your birth can modify their positions in the signs. But the most important consideration is your ascendant – the sign rising on the eastern horizon when you took your first breath – and its exact degree. Your ascendant greatly modifies the personal appearance (though your Sun sign has a lot to say about that, too) and it forms your true inner nature, upon which the motivations of your Sun sign are based. If your ascendant is Leo, for example, you may have strong Leo leanings, and wonder why the descriptions of your Aquarius Sun sign don't include all of your idiosyncrasies and secret longings. The two most important positions in any natal chart, after the Sun sign, are the ascendant and the Moon sign.

You'll find it interesting to obtain your ascendant from an astrologer (which can be done quickly over the telephone), and then read the description for that sign, along with your regular Sun sign. You'll find that the two of them blended make up your total personality to a remarkable degree. A third blending of your Moon sign with the other two will give you an even more complete picture.

Next, the houses of the horoscope must be considered. These are mathematically computed locations in the natal chart which have influence over different areas of your life. There are twelve of them, one for each sign. The first house is always ruled by the sign on your ascendant, and so on, in counter-clockwise order around the circle which forms the horoscope. The astrologer who has carefully calculated your natal chart, based on the exact time of your birth and its geographical location, must interpret the meaning of each sign's influence on these houses – or locations – also taking into consideration the planets which fall into their specified areas. Blending all the foregoing factors in analysing your character, your potential, and the indications of your past and future mistakes and possibilities (which are based on the aspects of the progressed and transiting planets to your natal planet positions) is called the art of synthesis in astrology. That's what takes the time, talent, effort and knowledge of the astrologer. Calculating the chart itself is a relatively simple task, once certain mathematical formulas are followed.

But back to your Sun sign, because, after all, that's what this book is about. In a way, saying that you're an Aquarian is rather like saying you're from New York, which isn't the generalization it seems to be. Wouldn't it be fairly easy to spot a Texan in a New York bar – or a New Yorker in a Texas restaurant? Isn't there a considerable difference between a Georgian politician and a Chicago industrialist? Of course. A rather marked difference.

Imagine that you're a Texan, discussing a man who is about to arrive for a business meeting. Someone says, 'He's a New Yorker,' and immediately an image is formed. He'll probably have faster, more clipped speech than a Texan, be less warm in his personal relationships, and will want to plunge into business without too many preliminary pleasantries. He'll probably be in a hurry to get the contracts signed and catch a plane back to the east coast. He'll be sophisticated to some degree, and probably more liberal than the Texan in his politics. Why is this instant impression likely to be pretty accurate? Because the New Yorker lives a fast life in a fast city, where slow reactions may lose him the seat on the subway or the taxi in the rain. He's constantly rubbing shoulders or elbows with the famous, so he's not easily awed. He has access to the latest plays and the best museums, so it's hard for him to remain unsophisticated. Due to higher crime rates and crowded living conditions, he won't be as hospitable or as interested in his neighbours as the Texan – his personality will be somewhat cooler.

Of course, a New Yorker can be a slow-talking Taurean or a slow-moving Capricorn, but he wouldn't be quite as slow as the Texan Taurean or Capricorn, would he? Nor would a fast-thinking and acting Gemini be quite as fast if he lived in Texas as he would if he lived in New York. It's all relative.

All right, he's a New Yorker. Now assume you discover he's Italian. Another image. He's a writer for television. A third image. He's married, with six children – and yet another dimension of the man is revealed. Therefore (although this is an analogy, and all analogies are imperfect), saying he's a New Yorker is like saying he's an Aquarian, for instance, and adding the further information is comparable to knowing that his Moon was in Virgo and he had a Scorpio ascendant when he was born, etc. But even without the extra knowledge, just knowing that he's a New Yorker puts you considerably ahead of those who don't know if he's from Tibet or the South Sea Islands. In the same way, even without a natal chart, just knowing a man is an Aquarian or a Leo can give you more understanding of him than could ever be possessed by those who don't know if they're coping with a fiery Sagittarius or an earthy Taurus.

It's true that a detailed nativity can infallibly reveal the finer nuances of character. It can indicate marked inclinations towards or against dope addiction, promiscuity, frigidity, homosexuality, multiple marriages, a disturbed childhood, alienation from or neurotic attachments to relatives, hidden talents, career and financial potential. It can show clearly tendencies to honesty or dishonesty, cruelty, violence, fears, phobias and psychic ability; plus many other strengths and weaknesses of inner character which may be latent for years, then burst forth under provocation during planetary progressions and transits which affect the natal planet positions for a temporary period of time. Susceptibility and immunity to accident and disease are revealed, secret attitudes towards drink, sex, work, religion, children, romance – and the list could go on and on. There are no secrets hidden from the accurately calculated natal chart. None except your own decision concerning how much of your individual free will you may decide to exercise.

However, in the absence of such a complete analysis, everyone can profit from a study of Sun signs, and the knowledge can make us more tolerant of one another. Once you understand how deeply ingrained certain attitudes are in people's natures, you'll become more sympathetic towards their behaviour. Learning Sun signs can help cool, poised Scorpio parents to be more patient with the quick brightness they would otherwise think was restless fidgeting in a Gemini child. It helps extroverted students understand introverted teachers, and vice versa. You'll forgive the Virgo his pickiness when you realize he was born to keep every hair straight and to untangle issues by examining each detail. It's easier to bear the carelessness of the Sagittarian when you understand he's too busy finding causes to cherish and defend to look where he's going every minute or notice whose toes he's stepping on. His frankness will cut less when you're aware of his compulsion to speak the truth, whatever the cost.

You won't be as hurt when a Capricorn doesn't 'ooh' and 'ah' over the gift you gave him, after you've remembered that he's deeply grateful, but incapable of showing his pleasure openly. His insistence on duty will chafe less when you know that he disciplines himself as severely as he does others. Putting up with the endless Libran arguments and hesitations is somehow more bearable with the Sun sign knowledge that he's only trying to be fair and reach an impartial decision. The Aquarian won't seem as rude when he roots into your private life if you stop to think he was created with an uncontrollable urge to investigate people's motives.

Once in a great while you may come across a Leo, for example, with, say, five or six planets in Pisces. The Piscean influences will obviously project themselves strongly, making his Sun sign harder to guess, since they'll greatly subdue his Leo qualities. But that will happen only rarely, and if you're completely familiar with all twelve Sun signs in detail, he can't disguise his true nature forever. No matter how hard the fish tries to hide the lion, that Leo Sun sign will never be totally eclipsed – and you'll catch him unawares.

Never make the mistake of skimming the surface when you're trying to recognize Sun signs. Not all Capricorns are meek, not all Leos are outwardly domineering and not all Virgos are virgins. You'll find an occasional Aries with a savings account, a quiet Gemini or even a practical Pisces. But look beyond the one or two traits that threw you off. You'll catch that flashy Capricorn peeking at the social register – the shy Leo pouting over a slight to his vanity – and the rare flirtatious Virgo buying insecticide by the case, because it's cheaper. The quiet Gemini may not talk fast, but her mind can operate at jet speed. The exceptional thrifty Aries will wear a bright-red Mars coat to the bank or talk back to a rude bank clerk – and the practical Pisces secretly writes poetry or invites six orphans for dinner every Thanksgiving. No one can successfully hide his or her Sun sign from you, if you keep your eyes and ears open. Even your pet will show unmistakable Sun sign traits. Don't move the food dish of a Virgo cat to a strange spot – and never try to ignore a Leo dog.

It's fun to practise with famous people, politicians, fictional heroes and heroines. Try to guess their sign, or what sign they most represent. It sharpens your astrological wits. You can even try comic strip characters. Good old Charlie Brown is obviously a Libran, and Lucy could only be a Sagittarius with an Aries ascendant and her Moon in Virgo. As for Snoopy, well, anyone can easily see he's an Aquarian dog, the way he wears that crazy scarf and the World War I aviator's cap, while he chases an imaginary Red Baron from the roof of his dog house. (Snoopy may also have an afflicted Neptune.) Try it yourself, and you'll have lots of fun. But what's more important, as you play the Sun sign game, you'll be learning something very serious and useful: how to recognize people's hidden dreams, secret hopes and true characters – how to understand their deepest needs – how to like them better and make them like you – how to really know the people you know. It's a happier world, and people are pretty great, when you look for the rainbows hidden inside them.

Isn't that really life's major problem? Understanding? Abraham Lincoln said it simply and clearly: 'To correct the evils, great and small, which spring from positive enmity among strangers, as nations or as individuals, is one of the highest functions of civilization.'

Start right now to study your Sun signs, use reasonable caution when you apply them, and people will wonder where you got all your new perception when you begin to unmask their real natures. In fact, understanding the twelve Sun signs will literally change your life. You're on your way to understanding people you've never even met. You'll soon feel closer to strangers, as well as to friends, and isn't that really rather wonderful?

It's nice to know you . . .

Linda Goodman

'Twas brillig, and the slithy toves
Did gyre and gimble in the wabe:
All mimsy were the borogroves,
And the mome raths outgrabe.

AQUARIUS
the Water Bearer

21 January to 19 February

How to Recognize Aquarius

'In spring, when woods are getting green,
I'll try and tell you what I mean:
In Summer, when the days are long,
Perhaps you'll understand the song:'

'For this must ever be
A secret
Kept from all the rest
Between yourself and me.'

Lots of people like rainbows. Children make wishes on them, artists paint them, dreamers chase them, but the Aquarian is ahead of everybody. He lives on one. What's more, he's taken it apart and examined it, piece by piece, colour by colour, and he still believes in it. It isn't easy to believe in something after you know what it's really like, but the Aquarian is essentially a realist, even though his address is tomorrow, with a wild-blue-yonder postal code.

Like the bewildered Alice, taken through the maze of Wonderland by Aquarian Lewis Carroll, you'll have to be constantly prepared for the unexpected with Uranians. Generally kindly and tranquil by nature, Aquarians nevertheless enjoy defying public opinion, and they secretly delight in shocking more conventional people with occasional erratic conduct. These normally soft-spoken and courteous souls can suddenly short-circuit you with the most amazing statements and actions at the most unpredictable times. The typical Uranian is half Albert Schweitzer and half Mickey Mouse. His feet can be wearing sandals, boots, Oxfords or Hush Puppies, and he'll seldom bother to check whether they're appropriate for the occasion. He'll show up barefoot if he feels like it, and laugh at you for laughing at him. Aquarians often deliberately adopt weird attire to show their refusal to conform.

You can often recognize people born under this fixed, air sign by their frequent use of the word friend. Aquarian Franklin Roosevelt's fireside chats invariably began with, 'My friends . . .' and the typical Uranus question after a broken romance is, 'Can't we still be friends?' Aquarius is neither jaded nor naïve, neither enthusiastic nor blasé. Continuous experimentation simply leaves him curious to penetrate the next mystery, and the next mystery could be you. That person who seems to be either a million miles away mentally, or else dissecting you under an invisible microscope, is probably an Aquarian. It can be disconcerting to discover, after all his intense, flattering curiosity, that he's just as deeply interested in the personal lives of the corner policeman, the bartender, the bellboy, the nightclub singer or the inmates of the funny house, as he is in yours. Politics fascinate him, sports absorb him and children intrigue him. But then so do horses, automobiles, elderly people, medical discoveries, authors, astronauts, alcoholics, pianos, pinwheels and prayers – not to mention baseball and the late Louis Armstrong. Join the crowd and toss your ego in the wastebasket, or his coolly impersonal approach will be sure to bruise it.

Look for a strange, faraway look in the eyes, as if they contained some kind of magic, mysterious knowledge you can't penetrate. Aquarius eyes are typically vague, with a dreamy, wandering expression, and often (but not always) blue, green or grey. The hair is frequently straight and silky, likely to be blonde, sandy or light brown; the complexion is pale and the height is usually taller than average (though the ascendant can modify the appearance of any Sun sign). You'll notice a marked nobility of profile. Uranus features are finely chiselled, suggestive of Roman emperors cut on old gold coins. True Aquarians will often adopt the pose of the drooping head when they're thinking about a problem, or just after they've asked a question. The head drops abruptly forward, or cocks to one side, waiting for your reaction. Curiously, thanks to the dual sexuality of Uranus, there are often feminine characteristics in the male bodies, such as broad hips, for example – and masculine characteristics in the female body, such as broad shoulders.

Freedom-loving Uranians can be acutely funny, perverse, original, conceited and independent, but they can also be diplomatic, gentle, sympathetic and timid. The Aquarian will almost desperately seek the security of crowds and saturate himself with friendship. Then he'll fall into a gloomy, morose spell of loneliness, and want to be strictly left alone. But whether he's mingling or singling, he'll retain his sharp perception, which is at once both deeper and quicker than others. Uranus makes him a natural rebel, who instinctively feels that all old customs are wrong, and that drastic alteration and revolutionary change is what the world and people need (although if he's in politics, he's clever enough not to broadcast his views prematurely and spoil his strategy).

To this end, Aquarians are always analysing situations, friends and strangers. It can be disturbing when they start asking point-blank questions, with a bare minimum of tact, as they probe into the heart of your private feelings. When they discover the puzzle wasn't so complex after all, they become bored, sometimes even upset. Nothing is more insulting than to have an Aquarian tire of his game of microscopic examination and turn to the next interesting person, just when he's convinced you he thinks you are the most important human being on earth. It stings.

Despite their fixation on friendship, Aquarians don't have many intimates. They seek quantity rather than quality in their associations, and they seldom settle down to a steady relationship for more than a limited period. There's too much to discover around the next corner to remain tied to one or two friendships exclusively. It does little good to make an emotional appeal to such an impersonal nature, but if you touch the heart of an Aquarian (which is not the same thing as mere emotion), he'll usually get off his bicycle and come back to see what he might have missed.

A peculiar sort of isolation hangs over the Uranian, and he's often misunderstood by mankind. That's because mankind hasn't yet caught up with the Aquarian Utopia. Since the water bearer lives in the future, coming back only briefly to the present, he can seem just plain pixilated to more mundane souls. He senses this, and it deepens his sense of isolation. But just because others can't keep up with him is no reason in his opinion to go backwards. So he wanders among his lonely clouds, while we mere mortals wonder what he's doing out there. Astrology teaches us that 'As the Aquarian thinks, so will the world think in fifty years.' That may be true, but it certainly doesn't narrow the gap between the Uranus-ruled and the rest of us today. This Sun sign is known as the sign of genius, and so it is, since over seventy per cent of the people in the Hall of Fame are either Sun Aquarians or have Aquarian ascendants. On the other hand, a substantially high percentage of those confined in mental institutions, or who drop in for regular couch sessions with an analyst, are also Aquarians. There's a fine line, they say, between genius and insanity, and your Uranian friends can sometimes make you wonder which side of the line they're on. A great deal of the confusion is due to man's tendency to belittle his prophets. The familiar quotes that 'they laughed at Fulton and his steamboat', 'they thought Edison was mentally retarded', and 'they wanted to lock up Louis Pasteur', are examples of the attitude of the materialistic world towards those whose senses are tuned to higher spheres of thought.

Uranians are a curious mixture of cold practicality and eccentric instability, and they seem to have an instinctive empathy with the mentally disturbed. It's a curious fact that almost any Aquarian can substantially reduce the anxiety of the insane simply by talking to them quietly. He has a marvellous knack of calming hysterical people and soothing frightened children. It is because of his own thinly covered, highly acute nervous system that he has such deep understanding.

The Aquarian outlook is so broad that you'll seldom find one who is prejudiced, unless there are severe planetary influences in the natal chart. Even then, he'll be deeply shocked when his prejudice is pointed out. The brotherhood instinct is so strong in him that when a rare Aquarian is guilty of being intolerant, he's not only unaware of it, he hates the label. Ordinarily, everyone is his brother or sister. He'll wander through affluent society and the slums alike with his symbolic jar, gathering the waters of knowledge and pouring them out again, except

for those occasional lapses into hibernation. But his hiding
out periods seldom last long, and before you get a chance
to miss him, the Uranian is back gregariously making the
rounds again. Don't try to interrupt his solitude. When
he wants to be alone, he wants to be alone, but he hasn't
retired from the mainstream permanently, even if he does
take a sudden Uranus notion to get an unlisted phone
number. His address hasn't changed, and neither has he.
He can never renounce people for long. Ignore him and
he'll soon be walking around town on those home-made
stilts, as alert and inquisitive as ever.

Ordinarily, it's difficult to get an Aquarian to make a
precise appointment. He'd rather keep it loose, because
he doesn't like to be pinned down to specific duties or
obligations at specific times. He prefers a casual 'I'll see
you around – maybe some time Tuesday' to a definite
hour for a meeting. (And he sometimes means the second
Tuesday of next week.) However, I will say that, once
you've succeeded in nailing him and he gives you his word
he'll meet you at a particular hour, he will be there on
the dot. You can count on it, even set your watch by his
punctuality, and you'd better not be late yourself. He'll
show up dependably, unless he's been kidnapped on the
way (which, being an Aquarian, he could be. Anything
can happen to these people at any time. I mean but
anything).

You can expect him to give his opinion frankly, but he
won't try to dictate how you should think or how you
should live your life. Conversely, he doesn't intend to let
you tell him how he should think or live his. Unlike Aries
and Leo or Gemini, he has no desire to hard sell his ideas
to others. The Aquarian philosophy is that everyone has
his thing, his special yearning. Each person dances to his

own fiddle music, and individuality should be respected. It's interesting to see that, as the world moves into the Aquarian Age, the heralds of the new era are the flower people and the Gurus. In exaggerated fashion, they are simply reflecting the Aquarian ideals: equality – brotherhood – love for all – live and let live – seek the truth – experiment – and retire to meditate.

You'll rarely find the Aquarian fighting fiercely for a cause. They live their code, and feel that's enough. Let Aries, Scorpio, Leo and Sagittarius grab the sword and battle gloriously to free the downtrodden. The Uranus-ruled souls are too busy figuring out the reason for the revolution, listening to people's troubles and sharing sympathetic understanding. Aquarius believes in violent change, but he leaves the violence to others. He's not a moral or a physical coward. He just isn't geared for battle. When a fight catches him unawares, he may strike out blindly in confusion, or he may simply agree, to end the argument. His reaction is unpredictable, but one thing is certain. The next day his opinion will be as fixed as it was before. Anyone skilled in debate can usually get the best of him, since his attention can so easily wander to the abstract in a battle of wits. The Aquarian fights best with his hat. He puts it on and leaves. His truth-respecting mind, however, won't budge an inch when he has a firm conviction, despite his distaste for unpleasant confrontations. All the shouting and emotional pressure in the world won't keep him from determinedly going his own way with his independent ideas, while the fireworks explode all around him. The two Aquarian Presidents, Abraham Lincoln and Franklin Roosevelt, demonstrated this principle perfectly. The concepts were equally original and strikingly unpopular in both cases. There was no aggressive insistence on personal theories, yet the sweeping reforms were made, regardless of lack of co-operation and bitter opposition.

Another reason why Uranians often meet with hostile criticism is that they're so full of surprises. They can lead you west, then suddenly turn and march east, without warning. Aquarius has an obstinate way of not letting you know what he's up to. For weeks, the February-born father of a friend of mine ignored his wife's complaints about a stove that didn't work. He buried himself in his newspaper, oblivious to her desperate hints. Suddenly one day, a truck pulled up, two men unloaded a brand new stove, and connected it in the kitchen under the surprised eyes of his wife, who should have learned to expect such behaviour.

Trusting people doesn't come naturally to the Aquarian, until after he's scrutinized your motives, even your soul, if possible. It's easy to grow restive under his intent analysis of your every word and gesture. You get the feeling it's all being filed away in that penetrating mind for future reference, and it is. He may seem to be in a dreamy fog now and then, but don't you believe it. He can probably tell you how many eyelashes you have. Never expect the Uranian to take you at face value. His innate courtesy will never keep him from shining the Uranus spotlight on you, from head to toe. He wants to know what's behind that face, and he'll ask some mighty embarrassing questions to find out. But it's comforting to know that, once you're accepted, he'll be loyal, and his friendship will be unshaken by malicious gossip. If you're his real friend, he won't believe the nasty whispers of your enemies, although he'll undoubtedly listen to them out of sheer curiosity. Rest assured, however, that he'll make up his own mind in the final analysis.

Uranus illnesses are usually connected with the circulatory system. Aquarians shiver and shake in the winter, and suffer with the humidity in the summer. They're susceptible to varicose veins and hardening of the arteries in old age, if their emotions are directed into negative channels, and they tend to have accidents to the legs, especially the shin and ankles. The ankle bones are often weak, and there may be pains in the legs, due to poor circulation; frequent sore throats; and sometimes heart palpitation, usually not serious, unless there are severe afflictions in the natal chart. Uranians need lots of fresh air, sleep and exercise, but they seldom take advantage of these remedies. They don't get much fresh air because they close their windows, pile on the blankets and still complain that they're freezing. The high-frequency nervous tension that accompanies Uranus mental activity keeps them from getting enough sleep, and often the rest they do get is troubled by strange dreams. As for exercise, unless the Aquarian developed an early love of sports by playing football in his neighbourhood, it's difficult to prod him into moving fast, let alone running around the track. His mind gets a continual workout, but the body needs a strong push. Aquarian health is usually excellent in childhood, barring weird, Uranian complaints – impossible to diagnose. The real troubles don't begin until maturity increases stubbornness. These people are extremely susceptible to hypnosis. Intuitively, lots of them sense this and won't expose themselves to it for love nor money, but this is a mistake, because hypnotic suggestion from a good medical hypnotist could successfully remove their myriad phobias. They're acutely responsive to electrical treatment, too, which can be just as beneficial.

Aquarians don't have the best memories in the world, but then they really don't need to memorize much, since they seem to pick up knowledge out of thin air, with some kind of invisible antennae. Why should they clutter their minds with information they may never need, when they can reach out by osmosis and grasp just about anything they want? They're likely to come home from the store without the most important item on the grocery list, because they can't be bothered with remembering what is, to them, non-essential. The typical Aquarian is the embodiment of the legendary absent-minded professor. I know one who planned to meet his wife in front of the City Squire Motel at noon. But he arrived early and ran into an old friend. (Aquarians are always running into old friends. In Africa or the Aleutian Islands they will be sure to find somebody they know.) The Uranian was engrossed in conversation with his pal when his wife approached, all smiles. As she came closer he stared at her blankly, gallantly tipped his hat, then turned, took his friend's arm and walked down the street, deep in conversation, leaving the furious, frustrated woman standing on the corner, alone and forgotten.

The Uranus power of concentration can be awesome. Yet, they're also able to pick up things going on around and behind them when they choose, like a radar screen. They can carry on a complicated discussion and still not miss an inflection of what's happening in the other part of the room, if they decide to tune in. Sometimes you could swear the Aquarian paid no attention to anything you said, but the next day he'll repeat it back to you like a tape-recorder. Never underestimate the Uranian process of soaking up knowledge while they seem to be oblivious, even though now and then they get lost in concentration, like my friend who left his wife standing on the street, in a mood to kill.

What the Aquarius man or woman thinks is always a clue to tomorrow. The uncanny Uranus ability to plunge into the unknown and absorb mystical secrets without half trying leads to a peculiar sort of intuition which gives them a high degree of psychic precognition. I know one who literally answers the phone before it rings, and what's more, he knows who's on the other end before a word is spoken. Abraham Lincoln had several premonitions of his own death in startling detail. Almost every Aquarian has a unique kind of sensitivity that lets him know your inner desires. Without talk, he understands a need buried so deep that you're almost unaware of it yourself. Using that magical osmosis, the Aquarian can transmit his own thoughts with an unseen charge of electrical current. Even when his back is turned, he can project strong feelings by this strange process. During a long silence on the telephone, he may be sending and receiving vibrations when you think he's fallen asleep. Some Uranians don't need the GPO to send a telegram.

Yet, there's nothing superstitious about their thinking. A true scientist, even if he's a mechanic or a musician, the Uranian won't jump to a conclusion until it's passed the test of his keen mind. However, once he forms an opinion, it remains firmly fixed in his brain, and I do mean firmly. As strongly as he loves change in society and government, he won't change his own ideas one iota for anybody. He's completely open-minded about world progress, but his mind clamps shut when it involves his personal behaviour, which can be unexpectedly conservative. You can see that his liberalism has its boundaries.

Aquarians despise lying and cheating, and they avoid borrowing and lending. They'll give you money as a gift, but don't ask them for a loan. Did you ever try to touch Aquarian Jack Benny for a fast fifty? Jack may surprise you by saying yes, but be sure you pay him back promptly. A broken or a bad debt can put a wide crack in your friendship. Aquarians keep their word and pay their bills, and they expect others to do the same. Charge accounts don't normally excite them and credit cards can frighten them. All this love of honesty, however, can sometimes be distorted into questionable behaviour. As much as he hates hypocrisy and double-dealing, the Aquarian can somehow answer questions so cleverly that he gives a false impression. Yet he'll be outspokenly indignant if he catches anyone else guilty of such a delicate nuance of deception. He'll seldom tell an outright lie, but he can fool you in very subtle ways, which is hardly the essence of the honesty he so constantly preaches. His unrelenting search for truth and the desire to hide his own motives are incompatible traits, and the Aquarian must eventually face this inconsistency if he's going to learn the real truth about himself.

Aquarians get credit for being idealists, perhaps too much credit, for true idealism consists of blind faith and optimism, and the Uranian is too shrewd to fool himself with lost causes for long. He knows that most dreams are illusions, like the rainbow he has examined so closely and still loves. Tradition and authority leave him unimpressed. He'll politely respect them, but they won't stop his compulsive drive to uncover fallacies, distortions and illogical assumptions.

His mind and body must both be as free as the wind.

To try to pin down the Aquarian is to try to stabilize the butterfly, to stuff a spring breeze into a closet or confine a winter gale in a bottle. It can't be done, and besides, who in the world would want to try? Though he's so far ahead of his time that you have trouble catching his viewpoint immediately, it's still worthwhile to make the attempt. You'll always come away a little wiser, if a little bewildered. His astrological flower is the daffodil – and now you know the derivation of the world 'daffy'.

The soul of the water bearer is constantly torn asunder by Uranus, the unpredictable and violent planet of change which lets him see ahead with electric blue clarity to the future. Aquarius belongs to mankind. He represents its truest hopes and its deepest ideals. Even his metal, uranium, is not really a metal, but a radioactive, metallic chemical, found only in combinations. It's important in atomic research, and it can undergo continuous fission. The magnetic majesty of eight bolts of brilliant lightning reflected in the Aquarian sapphire can split open his secret for those who seek to know him – but only for an instant can you see into his lonely heart, long ago infused with Saturn's ancient wisdom – unless you too live in to-morrow.

Famous Aquarian Personalities

Francis Bacon	Charles Dickens	Jeanne Moreau
Alan Bates	Jimmy Durante	Paul Newman
Tallulah Bankhead	Thomas Edison	Kim Novak
John Barrymore	Mia Farrow	S. J. Perelman
Jack Benny	Clark Gable	Ronald Reagan
George Burns	Galileo	Vanessa Redgrave
Lewis Carroll	Jack Lemmon	Norman Rockwell
Katharine Cornell	Abraham Lincoln	Franklin Roosevelt
Charles Darwin	Charles Lindbergh	Ann Sothern
James Dean	Somerset Maugham	Adlai Stevenson

The Aquarius Man

All this time the Guard was looking at her,
first through a telescope,
then through a microscope,
and then through an opera-glass.
At last he said, 'You're travelling the wrong way,'
and shut up the window . . .

To wade bravely smack dab into the centre of the problem, don't expect an Aquarian male to behave the way
people in love are supposed to behave. If you do, you're
in for quite a jolt, maybe even a series of jolts. When it
comes to friendship, he's all you could ask for in a pal or
a confidant. Love? Well, as an Aquarian I once knew
said, 'Anybody can have a girl. But love is something else
again.' That was an astute observation. 'It's something
else', all right, with Aquarians.

It's when he acts as though he doesn't like you that
he's close to being hooked, and the reason is elementary –
simple logic. The Aquarian water bearer likes everybody.
Everyone is his friend. He'll even refer to his worst enemy
as 'my friend'. So it means something when he says he
doesn't like someone. Just what it means may take some
study. The various nuances can be complicated.

An Aquarian man doesn't want to reveal his true feelings, in spite of his favourite pastime of penetrating the
feelings of others. His own reactions and motives are complex, and he intends to keep them that way for the pure
pleasure of fooling you. Many strange experiences will

come to this man, through both love and friendship, and he'll scrutinize each one avidly. Until you get him to the altar, you're just another experience, another experiment, hard as that may be to take. Don't sniffle. He can be tricked, for all his caution. But before you start tricking him, you'd better try to understand how to cope with his unique outlook about people.

He's a group man, and teamwork comes naturally to him. Aquarius understands the fair play rules of sports as if he had invented them, and he carries these rules into his personal relationships. His interests are scattered all over the place. That's because his love of people is so impersonal; he gives a certain value to everyone he meets, while the rest of us save such efforts for only the very special people in our lives. To an Aquarian, everyone is special. And I mean everyone. Even those he hasn't met yet. Few Uranus men are either selfish or petty. When he does show those qualities, a gentle reminder that he's being narrow-minded will bring him around. Aquarius just can't stand to be called narrow-minded.

He responds to unusually high ideals, thanks to his rigid moral code (though you'd better understand that it's his own code, which may not necessarily reflect or correspond to the one accepted by society in general). He'll almost surely lead a life of change, controversy and unexpected events. Yet there will often be moments of perfect tranquillity with him, impossible to find with any other Sun sign. Once he's over the shock that he's allowed himself to become interested in one woman above all of mankind, he can be an extremely considerate lover. The danger area is before he's over the shock. Since he's so accustomed to neglecting his own problems in the interest of the majority, hopefully some of this attitude will rub off on his love life. Don't count on it, though. The chances are just as good that he'll suddenly realize he's devoting his complete loyalty to you, when there are all those other nameless faces out there who need him. Then he may lean over backwards to prove to himself that he hasn't lost his love for his friends and the rest of humanity by being attached to just one person.

Forever analysing, the Aquarian man will frequently ask himself, 'I wonder what she meant by that?' He won't rest until he finds out either. A puzzle drives him simply wild so don't be fooled by his nonchalance. When he senses something is hidden, he just won't sleep at night until he's unravelled the mystery and penetrated the veil. There's always the possibility that he might be disappointed in what he finds, so make sure it's worth discovering. If it isn't, he'll have no qualms about making it painfully evident – and off he'll go to unravel a new veil.

The girl who wants to land him eventually has first to intrigue him. An open book will never pique his curiosity. He's attracted to closed pages, the more tightly closed, the better to arouse his detective instinct. When a female either ignores him or keeps her own counsel, in the beginning at least, his eyes will open a little wider and he'll get an alert expression, amazingly like that of a bloodhound on the scent of something missing. Why is she so emotional? (You can be emotional, you see, as long as you don't explain why.) Is she really so changeable or is it an act? Why does she wear all that perfume and make-up and such low-cut dresses, and then get insulted when those Leos and Sagittarians and Scorpios whistle at her in front of the chemist's? Does she want male advances or doesn't she? Is she a puritan or promiscuous? What makes her tick? As he probes and questions and examines,

the girl is at first flattered, naturally – but when she sees
he's just as intently curious about the waitress who just
served them (not to mention the bus boy), she begins to
cool somewhat. Feeling like an insect trapped under a
scientist's cold eye isn't exactly calculated to cause the
heart to flutter in any feminine bosom. So she finally drifts
(or runs) away to a more fiery or earthy male, and the
Aquarian sadly sighs for an instant or two before he begins
his next romantic investigation. (If some new invention
or unique idea hasn't aroused his interest first. In which
case the next female research project must wait.)

Aquarian men can be touchingly gentle and docile, but
you'd better tie a bright-blue electric string around your
finger to remind you that his surface calmness is a mirage.
So is his apparent pliability. He won't tolerate an ounce
of opportunism from a female. If he thinks he's being
exploited, that unpredictable Uranian charm can vanish
so quickly you'll think Cary Grant has turned into James
Cagney, poised to throw a grapefruit-half in your face.
The frightening thing is that an extremely upset Aquarian
is perfectly capable of such shocking action. What's even
more frightening is that you may forgive him. Don't. At
least, not more than once. He admires a woman who
holds her ground, if she's not too masculine about it, and
if she lets him fly hither and yon, unencumbered by mushy
promises and tearful accusations. As for that grapefruit,
it's only fair to point out that Aquarians are usually most
gallant with the fair sex. But sometimes they can forget to
distinguish between the sexes in the throes of excitement.
Couple that with the Uranus unpredictability, and it does
add up to a possible squirt of grapefruit juice in the eye.

There's always an excellent possibility that an Aquarian
will achieve some sort of prestige during his lifetime. If

it's only a trophy for stickball or a brass plaque for being the tallest man in Succatosh County he's sure to be honoured with some kind of recognition. It could be something as splendid as winning the Nobel Prize. Lots of Aquarians achieve such distinctions. (On the other hand, a large percentage of disturbed Aquarians are weekly visitors to a head shrinker. It may be kind of tricky to tell the difference.)

Some Uranus-ruled men have a fetish for cleanliness. You may bump into one who shrieks if anyone uses his towel or breathes on his oatmeal. Behind this is an almost neurotic fear of germs and illness. The Aquarian isn't above letting his phobias trail over into his romantic life, when they can serve a purpose, though he may do so unconsciously. Don't be surprised if he complains that he's allergic to your eye shadow and it makes him sneeze. Uranians have a way of developing allergies to things they'd rather avoid, and they can even fool the doctors, let alone innocent, unsuspecting girls.

He's not the type to woo you with extravagant gestures. He's as likely to pull up a dandelion and toss it at you as bring you an orchid. To be honest, more likely. He won't present you with mink coats and diamonds. But life with him can still be glamorous, even without the mink. There's the well-known story about Helen Hayes and her husband, Charles MacArthur. When they first met, he handed her a bowl of peanuts and said, 'I wish they were emeralds.' Many years and many dollars later, he gave her a cluster of glittering emeralds with the remark, 'I wish they were peanuts.' I don't know if MacArthur was an Aquarian, but Uranus was certainly prominent in his natal chart. That's exactly the kind of unexpected glory you'll know with an Aquarian lover. Who needs mink?

Now let's face the worst fact courageously. No flinching or wishful thinking. Here it is. Unlike Cancer, Capricorn, Leo and Libra, Aquarians don't take to marriage like a baby takes to candy. To be truthful, most of them avoid it as long as it's humanly possible. A rare Aquarian male will be enticed into a shower of shoes and rice at an early age, but it doesn't happen often enough for the statistics to be encouraging. The way the impasse usually starts is that the Aquarian makes beautiful, wonderful, glorious friendship the basis of the love. (Easier to slide away from later, my dear.) They choose a girl who's also a chum, and who can keep up with the Aquarian interests, including Micky Mantle's batting average, crossword puzzles, Arabian horses, fireflies on the Mississippi and the Dead Sea Scrolls. Why? That's easy. With so much to talk about, there's less time for love-making, which can get him seriously involved and committed. His ideal is the female who is his friend, and who doesn't make heavy emotional demands on him. Where do we go from here? Nowhere, usually.

Aquarian men find it difficult to relax in physical expressions of love. That first goodnight kiss may be a long time materializing. Admittedly, it's often well worth waiting for, and the suspense makes it ever more special. But he'll cling to the illusion that he's involved in a nice, safe platonic friendship long after such a palsy-walsy relationship has become impossible for you.

Even after he's mustered the courage to say 'I love you', he'll avoid the issue of marriage with every excuse in the book. When those run out, he can think up some pretty imaginative new ones. He'll patiently explain that he can't support you in the manner you deserve, his parents need him at home, or he's not good enough for you. If that doesn't work, he'll claim that the future is too uncertain, what with the threats of nuclear destruction and all. What if his boss sends him to Alaska next year? You might die of pneumonia up there, and he would be grief-stricken the rest of his life. You think he can't top that? One Aquarian man I know was engaged for twelve years to a girl he wouldn't marry because 'she would have to sacrifice a great career on Broadway.' The fact that the girl had never set foot on a stage in her life was beside the point. *He* thought she had talent. Some day, a producer might just discover her. Then how would she feel if he had held her back by marrying her? Worse yet, how would he feel? Guilty. Just plain selfish and guilty. It's not surprising that this poor female finally escaped to a more positive rival.

But all is not lost. Though it's true that most Aquarians wed late, they do eventually wed – usually. It normally happens after the last bachelor friend has sailed away to a Bermuda honeymoon, and the Aquarian wakes up to realize that here is a mystery other people have solved that he hasn't even investigated. Naturally, he can't stand that, so pop goes the proposal! Suddenly, of course. Uranus, you know.

In the early stages, you may think he needs a lesson and decide to let him think he's lost you to a more aggressive suitor. Let me warn you that you're likely to stay lost. Your broken-hearted Uranian is not nearly as apt to come charging after you with the fire of possession in his eye as he is to shed a couple of quiet tears and say, 'Well, I guess the best man won.' He'll resign himself to a life without you with insulting ease. He's even liable to ask the unbearable question, 'Can't we still be friends?' If you say no emphatically, he'll probably just shrug dejectedly and slowly walk away. If you say yes – well, you're right back where you started – friends.

Jealousy isn't his cup of eggnog. He'll trust you until you show him you can't be trusted. Not because he's trusting by nature, but because his analytical dissection has already satisfied him about your character. Unless there are marked afflictions in his natal chart, he's not capable of unfounded suspicion and possessiveness. If he does have a rare stab of jealousy, you'll never know it if he can help it. He will rarely, if ever, be physically unfaithful himself, mostly because the whole subject of sex, though it's interesting, doesn't consume him. An occasional Aquarian may spend a great deal of time intensely pondering sex, but if you know one of these, you can safely assume there's a heavy Scorpio influence in his natal chart. (And chances are even this type won't pursue it actively and openly.)

Once an Aquarian has chosen a mate, he figures he can concentrate on more important things. He can relax and investigate the boy-girl or man-woman relationship at his own leisure in his own private laboratory (which isn't a bad possibility for its eventual chance of success when you stop to think about it).

Uranian sex is part of a larger image or ideal. Should a temptation to engage in illicit romance arise (illicit in his eyes, that is), he'll usually end the affair abruptly, though it may hurt him deeply, rather than continue what he considers to be a dishonest relationship. The situation that made him feel guilty could be almost anything, from the disapproval of your parents or conflicting religions to an old boy friend not completely discarded, a promise he made to himself at the age of eight, or something he once read in a book. But whatever it is, it will somehow have to be adjusted and resolved before he'll ever renew the closeness, even if the love is as fated as that of Victoria and Albert. The Aquarian will always let his heart break silently, lest his friends hear and ask questions.

He's capable of waiting until he's ninety to claim you, even if you feel that's a bit long to wait for consummation. The worst of it is that he'll never give a reason for the break. That's for him to know and you to find out. He'll perversely let you think it was just a fantasy from the beginning, and hold back the real truth that it was genuine for some hazy future day of forgiveness and reconciliation. It can be pretty cruel, but that's the way he plays the game.

Your only comfort is the knowledge that he's suffering in his own way, too. How will you know that? Read 'How to Recognize Aquarius' again. He has his subtle ways of telegraphing his feelings, and they can be enormously frustrating – especially when his unique, private communication signals a green go light while he publicly keeps holding out a red stop light until he's ready to switch. It can make for some nasty romantic traffic snarls. It's hard on the pedestrian, but he's in the driver's seat, so there's not a lot you can do – except perhaps think up another mystery to tempt him with, or maybe shake him a little with some smashing success to make him curious to talk with you again – like being the first woman to orbit Venus.

Not that such a feat will change his feelings. If he really loves you, he'll love you even if you don't orbit any further than to the corner delicatessen, but it might interfere with his fixed strategy. You may gather from all this that a Uranus man can be pretty stubborn when it comes to love. You would be so right. His fixity in affectionate matters can drive you straight into the booby hatch or

drive you to someone else in desperation. That's a big fat
waste of time. He's not jealous, remember? Or he won't
show it, if he is. Besides, with his darned Uranian
intuition, he'll know it's all an act. Because he knows
what makes you tick. Don't forget, he studied you for a
long time. About the only thing you can do is hope you'll
still be attractive at ninety or else start practising those
Venus orbits.

Putting the shoe on the other foot, an Aquarian can
arouse a heap of possessiveness in you, when the tables
are turned. Don't let it throw you off balance. Thanks to
the everlasting Uranus proclivity for friendship, whenever
and wherever he finds it, there may be times when you
won't know where he is, even after you're married and
you should. Just tell yourself that, no matter how late he
sits up with a friend, it's only his normal curiosity at
work, his never-ending interest in people. If the friend is a
woman, pretend you didn't notice. In all honesty, he most
likely didn't. You can expect the truth when you ask him
a direct question. But if you doubt him and ask again,
he'll figure you don't want the truth. To punish you, he'll
make up the wildest story he can dream up (and he can
dream up some pretty wild ones). You may regret your
suspicions when you spend a few hours in abject misery
wondering if he really did tell that redhead she was gor-
geous. (That's after he told you he didn't even remember
talking to her and you said, 'Ha! I just bet you don't
remember.') He honestly didn't, but you asked for details,
so he gladly obliged with some purely imaginary ones to
teach you a lesson. You'll learn fast.

Don't be hurt when he's in one of his solitary moods
and prefers to be alone with his silent dreams. He'll return
to share them with you, all the more warm and tender

for his spiritual retreat and anything that warms him up should definitely be encouraged.

He may not be the best breadwinner around, but he's capable of inventing something beneficial to the world or being the first man to land on Mars. He'll feel right at home there, too. There's always surprise just around the corner with an Aquarian husband, even when the budget is shaky. Naturally, there are a few Uranian men who are wealthy, even millionaires, but a high income bracket is seldom a burning ambition. All the rich Aquarians you see probably stumbled on it. It's certain they didn't greedily grasp for it. If he has a fat bank book, the chances are it gained weight while he was attempting to improve some product or idea for the good of humanity in general – or he's saved it to support his eccentric old age. Who knows? He might want to take a trip in a time machine some day, and he wants to be sure to have the fare. Most of the time he'll be reasonable about money, but save when you can, and don't run up charge accounts. He'll never recover from sheer extravagance on your part. Sometimes he can surprise you with a burst of generosity, but he won't go overboard unless he has an Aries, Leo, Sagittarius or Pisces ascendant. Even then, he won't be a big butter-and-egg man.

The children will find him the greatest listener on the block. He'll be fascinated at the perfect breath control of the wolf when he blew down the three little pigs' pad – and curious about how the old witch pickled the poisoned apple that put the whammy on Snow White. A small boy's trouble learning how to strike a home run and a little girl's tears over a broken doll are simply the problems of a couple of pals in trouble to an Aquarian father. He's a whiz at complicated arithmetic questions, too.

Don't let your career make you neglect to feed him or
sew on his buttons. Don't encourage your girl friends to
camp on his couch or tie up the telephone for hours, and
don't get engrossed in TV or a novel when he wants you
to find his old soft ball in the attic or pull a splinter out
of his finger. He married you for several reasons. Though
romance may play its part, the most important reason was
to have you around – so he would always have someone to
mash his baked potato, cross-stitch his buttonholes, find
his lost articles and operate on an occasional splinter. He
won't cotton to your letting television, reading or female
chums interfere with those duties. His idea of a good wife
and mother is quite simple: a woman who keeps at it
almost constantly. Even the more liberal Aquarian husbands will frown on a glamorous gadabout. But you won't
mind it too much. He's so full of interesting surprises
himself, you won't need soap operas, women's magazines
and tête-à-têtes with girl friends to keep your mind and
emotions challenged. (He may be about all the challenge
you can take.) You can always catch up on the female
gossip and such when he's engrossed in some new project
and gets a little absent-minded about what you're doing.
But just be sure to be there when he has a sore finger,
because he can be a real sorehead when he's neglected.

Strangely, since he's so realistic about most things, the
Aquarian will never forget his first love. (Not the first
date, but the first girl who ever gave him a rainbow.
There's a difference.) Uranians frequently marry childhood sweethearts years later, or cling to a faded illusion.
An Aquarian can usually describe his first love in detail,
which can be annoying to a wife. The solution is to be
that first love. You may have to wait a long time to wear
orange blossoms, but at least you won't be replaced by a

ghost. Who else could turn peanuts into emeralds or vice versa, never mind a little grapefruit juice in the eye? Despite his general romantic clumsiness, he can come up with sudden phrases which could only have been invented by the angels. He can forget your wedding anniversary, but he'll bring you violets in January. Christmas? Who says it has to be 25 December? It can be any time you want it to be. He may go for days or weeks or months without a single word of romance or affection. Then some morning while you're slicing his blueberry pie, he'll look deep into your eyes and ask gently, 'Do you know how beautiful you are?' There will be something about the way he says it that will make your knees weak.

Jingle bells on the seashore, birthdays at dawn, Valentine's Day on Hallowe'en, rainbows at midnight. Pin a red heart on an orange pumpkin, roll Easter eggs in the snow, light the candles on the cake on top of a Ferris wheel – you're in love with an Aquarian, didn't you know? I wish you a Frank Merriwell ending. But be careful. You can get lost out there in Wonderland.

The Aquarius Woman

But Alice had got so much into the way
of expecting nothing but out-of-the-way things to
happen
that it seemed quite dull and stupid
for life to go on in the common way . . .

Put cats in the coffee, and mice in the tea –
And welcome Queen Alice with thirty times three!

The safest way to enter into romance with an Aquarian female is to remember she's as paradoxical in love as she is in everything else. That way, you won't be expecting Priscilla Alden and get Pocohontas.

This girl has all the faithfulness of the fixed signs when she's in love, but she also has the detachment and lack of emotion of the air element. It's possible to have a happy relationship with the Uranus woman, if you leave her free to pursue her myriad interests and circulate among her friends. Never try to tie her to the stove or the bedpost. Ask the man who's tried. She can suddenly decide to study ballet, meditate in the mountains or join the Peace Corps. Remember the story of the princess with the long, golden hair, who lived high in a tower? That's the Aquarius female. Cutting off her flowing tresses won't change her, any more than it did in the fairy tale. She dreams different dreams than you or I. She hears a distant drummer – and follows a star most of us have never seen.

She belongs to everyone, and yet to no one. Her love

can be tender and inspired, but there will always be a vaguely elusive quality about it, like a half-remembered song. You can hum the melody, but the lyrics keep slipping away. The Aquarian girl's demand for freedom is insistent, but her allegiance to anyone who can accept romance within such limits is boundless. Here's something you'll like: she won't be terribly interested in your bank book (unless Cancer or Capricorn or Taurus is on her ascendant). Money is never the prime consideration of the typical Aquarian woman. She won't care if you're not the richest man in town, but she'll expect you to be respected in some way for your intellectual achievements. Dr Christian Barnard and his heart transplants or Werner von Braun and his rockets interest her far more than J. Paul Getty and his billions.

When you set out to catch this butterfly in your net, remember that she'll never spend her unpredictable life with a man who isn't true to himself. Her own code of ethics may be as weird as anything you've ever come across, and quite different from the accepted codes of society, but she lives up to it totally. She'll understand that your rules may also be highly individual. That's fine with her, but don't compromise those rules. If you're looking for a passion flower, you've picked the wrong daisy. Passion is not her forte, if she's a typical Aquarian. She'll think physical love is pleasant enough, if it's not overemphasized. In other words, she can take it or leave it alone. Uranus females can respond to lovemaking with a haunting, deep intensity, but if you prefer to keep it platonic for long periods of time, that's all right, too. Like all Aquarians, she may have an unconscious fear that desire for one person will imprison the spirit in some way, and keep her from being true to her one great love –

freedom. Freedom to experiment and investigate and freedom to give time to humanity. Also freedom to pursue her rather kicky, offbeat fancies.

She's an ideal girl if you're planning a political, scientific or educational career. You couldn't do better, unless you happen to run across an Aquarian girl with adverse planetary positions in her natal chart, who enjoys shocking people by walking barefoot down Main Street or smoking big, black cigars on buses. There are some pretty wild, way-out Uranian females here and there. But the average girl born under the sign of the water bearer is a social delight. She's graceful, witty, bright as a penny, and extremely adaptable to all forms of society, high and low and in the middle.

Her lack of suspicion under normal circumstances is a special bonus. A travelling salesman should find his dream girl in the typical Aquarian female. If she actually catches you being unfaithful, it will cause a deep wound to her sensitive nature. You'll know it the minute you look into those strange, dreamy eyes. But she won't suspect you without cause, and she'll rarely doubt your word. The typical Uranus woman will never check up on you after you leave, phone you at the office, inspect your handkerchiefs for lipstick stains or look for blonde hairs caught in your cuff link. Deception will have to be brought forcibly to her attention; she won't go out looking for it. Before you give her too much credit, consider that her lack of passionate jealousy is due to something more than strength of character. First of all, she probably dissected your psyche under a microscope before she gave you a second glance. Besides, she has so many outside interests and so many people who turn her on to talk with, there's not much time for her to worry about what you're doing when you're out of sight. Out of sight can often mean out of mind for Aquarians of both sexes. Absence seldom makes the Uranus heart grow fonder. Occasionally, an Aquarian woman will suffer a promiscuous or flirtatious mate, because there's something she needs which she can find only with him, so she looks the other way. On the other hand, if she doesn't really need you, that moral strength will work in reverse at the first actual proof of infidelity. She'll simply walk away. Don't try to kindle the embers, they're stone cold dead. Of course, you can still be friends. Why not? She's willing. It never embarrasses an Aquarian girl to be chummy with ex-lovers or husbands. She's forgotten the past and wiped the slate clean of memories.

There is one peculiar and notable exception to the rule. Like the Uranus man, the Uranian female will remember the first true and honest love for a lifetime. Only the first, however. Are you wondering whether that Aquarius girl you once knew still remembers you? The answer lies in her definition of love. It could have something to do with the first boy who gave her a bunch of sweet peas when she was nine – the boy who walked her through the park in the rain – or the one with the funny ears, who knew the clown at the circus, and used to feed her peanuts.

Uranus women involved in extra-marital affairs are rare. They can be tempted in exceptional situations, but a dishonest relationship goes against their chemistry. It won't be long until an undercover romance is broken off for good. Yet, there are many Aquarian divorcees. There's a reason. If a situation becomes intolerable, the Uranian nature turns cold suddenly. They can disappear overnight and never look back. They don't seek or enjoy divorce, but it isn't the shock to them it is to their more sentimental

sisters. Uranus rules change, you know. Since she's such
an individualist, with a list of friends several miles long,
the Aquarian female never hesitates to make her way
alone if the need arises.

Expect her to probe into your heart until you haven't
a secret left, or a dream that hasn't been analysed. But
don't try to dissect her private thoughts. That's not the
way the game is played with Aquarians. She'll keep her
motives hidden, and sometimes take a perverse pleasure
in deliberately confusing you. She'll usually be truthful to
a fault, but remember, with an Aquarian, telling a lie
is one thing. Refraining from telling the whole story is
another.

It's comforting to know that an Aquarian girl is pretty
cagey with a buck. That is, it's comforting to know unless
you're planning to hit her for a loan. She might say yes
once or twice, but if you let your credit rating slip, she
can be colder than the guy at the bank when you skip
your car payment. On the rare occasions when she accepts
a small loan herself, you'll get back every penny with no
stalling, excuses or feminine wiles, if she's a typical
Uranus female. As for every man's nightmare of charge
accounts, you'll have little worry on that score. Aquarian
women are uncomfortable about owing money. Bad debts
don't fit in with the Uranus code.

Her appearance is puzzling. Most Aquarian women
are lovely, with a haunting, wistful beauty. But they're
changeable. They can give an impression of smooth
whipped cream, then suddenly switch to salty pizza, as
quickly as a bright, blue, zig-zag bolt of Uranian electricity. Next to Librans, Aquarian females are often the
most beautiful women in the zodiac. At the very least,
they're interesting-looking. The Aquarian manner of

dressing can stop you dead in your tracks. There are a few of them who could grace the cover of a fashion magazine, but the average Aquarian girl is anything but conventional about her costumes. She can wear some outfits a gypsy would envy, and her naked individuality can produce some mighty unique combinations. She'll usually be the first to wear a new fad, no matter how zany it is, yet she can also stick to Grandma's styles – even great-grandma's styles. With typical Aquarian indifference, she'll mix yesterday's lace snood with today's metallic jump suit, and the effect can be a little startling. She'll wear her lace nightgown to a formal banquet, ostrich feathers to the supermarket, bell bottom slacks to the opera, sneakers to the theatre, diamonds when she visits the zoo – and top it all off with a faded Mother Hubbard she picked up in a thrift shop.

Your Aquarian girl will probably have an unusual way of wearing her hair. Her tresses are as unpredictable as her personality. They can be worn braided, pig-tailed, pinned in a bun, flowing down like a waterfall, short as a marine's, in Mary Pickford curls or as straight as a poker. One thing you can depend on. Her hair won't look like the hair of any other female on this planet.

A conversation with her can be remarkable, to say the least. She has charming manners, and usually behaves in a timid, almost reserved way. Then comes one of those sudden Uranus urges, and out will pop a remark with absolutely no relation to what anyone is saying. You'll be talking about the fluctuations of the stock market, and she'll interrupt out of nowhere with: 'Did you know that Woodrow Wilson, Jack Kennedy, Herbert Hoover, Harry Truman, Calvin Coolidge, Benjamin Harrison, Franklin and Theodore Roosevelt and William McKinley all have double letters in their names?' There's only one way to answer a question like that. Tell her she missed Millard Fillmore, Ulysses Grant and Thomas Jefferson. Then gently, but firmly, lead the discussion back to the stock market. Other minds may progress in fairly logical steps, but hers zigs into tomorrow, then zags back into today with no more sense of direction than a flash of lightning. Now and then she'll toss off an unexpectedly poignant phrase. You'll ask her what she thinks of space travel and she'll answer, 'When I was a little girl, I thought the stars were holes in the floor of heaven where the light shone through.' If she's in a different mood, you'll say that melted snowmen make you sad, and she'll counter with: 'A melted snowman is just a pile of slush, Charlie.' First misty – then practical. First timid – then rowdy. Aquarian women will rudely ridicule flying saucers, then tell you a story about a polka-dotted elf on a windowsill. Never talk down to an Aquarian female. She'll resent not being considered your equal, and an unsympathetic attitude will cause her to retreat and become unapproachable.

Since Uranus rules the future, you might imagine that these girls would be natural mothers. Children do, after all, belong to the future. But the average Aquarian woman may be bewildered by motherhood in the beginning. She has to adjust to devoting all her attention and energy exclusively to one human being for a period of time, when she's used to spreading herself far and wide, and this can take some practice. Her natural aloofness may make it difficult for her to demonstrate warm affection outwardly. The typical Aquarian mother is devoted to her offspring, but also somewhat detached toward them. But she'll probably be the most willing PTA worker in the neighbourhood. She'll talk happily for hours with their small friends on their own level without patronizing them, and she'll give up her afternoons to work for a school project. The children will learn the lessons of brotherhood and humanity from her by observation. Aquarian mothers are never fiercely protective of their children. They take a tolerant view of the most startling confession. A Uranus woman will seldom punish a child for telling the truth, no matter what he's done. With her unprejudiced viewpoint, she'll gain the complete confidence of her little ones. She's great at reassuring young minds about everything from monsters hiding under the bed to the pain of being ignored in the playground. She can turn their tears to laughter in minutes. Your children will find her jolly fun, a little helter-skelter, relaxed about housework, helpful with homework and gentle when they're ill. She won't smother them with affection, and she'll seldom nag. Maybe Tommy didn't wash his hands the third time he was told, but she's more interested in what he learned in science class.

We may be a little ahead of ourselves. Even though Uranus likes to reverse the existing orders of things, before your Aquarian girl becomes a mother, she has to become a wife. And before she becomes your wife, you'll have to convince her that marriage isn't synonymous with Devil's Island. She won't exactly rush into matrimony. She's in no hurry to take your name until she's weighed you, sorted you, tested you, and found out what makes you tick. The opinions of her friends and family will mean nothing, though she may ask them what they think out of curiosity. She has her own yardstick for measuring you. Assuming you pass her test, marriage to an Aquarian girl can be confusing. She'll listen pleasantly when you give her advice, but there's something in the Uranian make-up that prevents her from following directions explicitly. She can't stick to the recipe when she bakes one of her angel fool cakes any more than she can park the car exactly where you told her to. There's some kind of a snag in her thinking that causes her to believe just a little twist will improve anything. But she'll smile agreeably as she goes on her own, sweet way. There's a constant urge to experiment with a different way to make the coffee, fill her pen, fasten her ice skates or cross the street. She'll wear a sweater backwards, mix her brandy with milk, arrange flowers in a fish bowl, rinse her hair in shaving lotion or make a rock garden on your desk. But don't ask her why. She doesn't know herself. The unique and unusual is her wavelength, that's all.

Because her nature is so impersonal, expressions of deep feelings won't come easily. Except for those sudden remarks that sound like a combination of Robert Frost and Yogi Berra, she has few words with which to express her love, and her pattern of physical passion is woven closely with threads connected to the mind and soul. Although the unique Uranus outlook leads some Aquarian girls into peculiar attachments, once they find the right mate, their marriages are usually models of happiness.

Your Aquarian woman can float through her days and nights with all the grace of a proud swan, but she may behave like a clumsy bear in romantic situations. The line between friendship and love is often all but invisible to Aquarius. Love songs about people who only have eyes for each other strike her as silly. There are so many miracles in the world for eyes to behold, it seems to her a terrible waste for two pairs of them to do nothing but gaze into each other's depths. She'll be glad to let you take her hand and walk beside her as she looks with happy delight on the sunrise, an antique car, the milkman's horse, a yellow garbage pail, a stuffed owl or a red balloon caught in a church steeple. But don't distract her with too much togetherness. Let her wander through her wonderland alone when she chooses, and she'll never question your pinochle games with the boys.

The quickest ways to lose her are to show jealousy, possessiveness or prejudice; to be critical, stuffy or ultra-conservative. You'll also have to like her friends, who will come in odd, assorted sizes and shapes.

She's susceptible to sudden flashes of inspiration, and her intuition is remarkable. Her judgement may not seem sound or practical at first, because she sees months and years ahead. The Aquarian girl lives in tomorrow, and you can only visit there through her. What she says will come true, perhaps after many delays and troubles, but it will come true. I suppose, after all, that's the most special thing about your February woman. She's a little bit magic.

The Aquarius Child

The dream-child moving through a land –
Of wonders wild and new,
In friendly chat with bird or beast –
And half believe it true.

According to Mother Goose, if your offspring is dressed in blue, he's made of snips and snails and puppy-dog tails. If baby is wearing pink, she's made of sugar and spice, and everything nice. But if he or she was born in February, dress him in an aquamarine cap and electric-blue booties and forget that old rhyme. This infant is made of the raw material of Uranus, and he's going to make you chase him into tomorrow.

He's a quivering, sensitive, stubborn, independent mass of invention and electrical impulses. Even if he has a slow and careful Taurus ascendant, his mental processes will be as fast as Uranian lightning. His thoughts will vibrate like high frequency radio beams, and as he grows up, you may feel like sending out an SOS yourself.

Every mother and father think their child is special – different and unique, compared to other youngsters. But this one is just ridiculous. Lots of parents of a young Aquarian puzzle whether to send him out on the farm, where he won't frighten neighbours, or let the word casually get around that he may win the Pulitzer prize some day. Which route should you take? You have a problem. Yes, you do. The Pulitzer is possible, but my advice would be to try the farm for a few summers and watch. Observe.

Wait. He's liable to invent a new plough, or just eat them out of house and home. It depends. There's never a cut and dried rule with Aquarians.

I know one New York mother who just called her Uranian son 'the Bronx Wonder' and let it go at that. At least her relatives and neighbours were as mystified as she was. Nobody knew if the nickname meant he had three heads or he was headed for the Hall of Fame. As it turned out, he was a pretty good basketball player, and most folks thought that's why he had the tag. But they shouldn't have been so hasty. The story's not over yet. He's presently rotating between composing the score for a musical which may go on Broadway or in the wastebasket, playing bit parts in detective films, and making himself available for TV commercials. (The kind that need men-from-Mars types for flying saucer approaches on soft-sell automobile spots.) He's also working on an invention in his bedroom (between watching the Mets play and eating pickle sandwiches), but since he won't tell anyone what it is, I can't give you any clues. He has a kind of thing about clocks and watches, so it may have something to do with a time machine (a common Aquarian obsession). Well, we'll see. There's no rush. Lots of Aquarians don't break loose and shower electric sparks of genius on a waiting world until they're a young fifty. It makes it all a little nerve-racking, waiting around like that. Of course, there are quite a few Aquarian child prodigies, but we're tangled up enough trying to figure out your average Aquarian youngster (and I use the term average loosely).

He may end up working for the FBI or a private eye outfit (he loves to figure out mysteries), and become an ordinary, sensible, conservative citizen. (Don't hold your breath, but it's a possibility.) We'd better concentrate on his tender years. That way, you'll have a fighting chance to guide this Uranus rocket in some kind of direction.

Until maturity has mellowed Uranian influences, and society has moulded more conventional attitudes, an Aquarian youngster can be strongly negative. The immediate reaction to a command (or even a pleasant suggestion) is often an emphatic no. But let him think about it, mull it over, and it's surprising how many times his final reaction will be sensible – the answer he found by himself correct and acceptable.

These boys and girls can be calm and sweetly docile on the surface, but the north wind can turn them suddenly topsy turvy. (Except that, with an Aquarian, it could be turvy topsy. You can expect anything.) Unpredictable in their behaviour, but loveable and often amusing, the February child can be quite a spinning propeller to contend with. I used that analogy because Aquarians and Uranus rule air flight, planes and Charles Lindbergh and things like that. Yet, these youngsters are so full of contradictions, instead of taking to flight naturally, many of them have a strange, unreasonable fear of planes and elevators – even electricity (also ruled by Uranus). It isn't easy to direct them or channel them. They have no idea where they're going, but they have definite ideas about how to get there.

Raising and teaching these 'wonders' can be a big responsibility. Their minds combine fixed practicality with uncanny perception and sharp, probing logic. Mix it all up and it can be acutely embarrassing, like when your little Aquarian asks your best friend why she got her face lifted (she did) – or asks your Uncle Elmer why he cheated on his income tax in front of the Inland Revenue man (he did).

They love to do favours for friends. Buy your little Aquarian boy a brand new pair of boots, and he's likely to wear them out the first day – smoothing down the snow to make it slick so the neighbourhood kids can use their sleds.

Expect your February child to have a dream and hold it fast – until he gets another one. With a girl, it's likely to be a projection of herself as a prima ballerina, with a pure dedication to her art that would put Pavlova to shame, a thirst to be the first woman president or a hunger to follow in the footsteps of Madame Curie. With the boys, it could be an oceanographer, ichthyologist, archaeologist, anthropologist, an exterminator or a tree surgeon. Normal career choices like nurses, secretaries, clerks, salesmen, teachers, bankers and brokers are too mundane for the average Aquarian child's fantasies. He may have to settle for one eventually, but the original dream will be tucked under his left ear and not forgotten. It's eerie, but Aquarians can sometimes cause a thing to happen by simply concentrating on it and waiting.

You'll never know quite what to expect from day to day. This is a child who may not want to stay indoors when it rains. He'll be out with your best sterling-silver tablespoon, digging a drain so the hill in back of the house won't wash away.

Remember the old verse you heard as a child that went, 'The bear went over the mountain – the bear went over the mountain – the bear went over the mountain – to see what he could see. The other side of the mountain – the other side of the mountain – the other side of the mountain – was all that he could see.' Your Aquarius youngster will have better luck. He'll find something there. Maybe it will be a pot of gold or just a new species of woodpecker, but none of his exploratory journeys will ever result in a dead end or a total loss.

I skipped over the infant stage because these children are never infants. They are born middle-aged. However, many of them do go through the toddler stage, and during that precarious period you might be wise to consider buying a seeing-eye dog. Keep the dog until your little Uranian is at least ten. He may have trouble navigating the block without an incident. Off on his own private cloud, he'll lope down the street in a fog, and ram right into a telephone pole or a mailbox. Aquarian absent-mindedness brings on twisted ankles, broken bones and the wrath of teachers. You may be torn between pride, when the school reports he or she is a budding genius — and shame, when you receive a note saying, 'Oliver simply won't pay attention in class. He stares out the window all day and plays with his two-way wristwatch.' Or 'Gertrude refuses to concentrate. Instead of studying, she just sits there and flexes her arches in those silly ballet slippers.' A lecture to Oliver and Gertrude will result in a shrug of bored impatience. What's all the fuss about? He was trying to figure the effect of the summer solstice on Greenwich Mean Time, and she was wondering what makes a worm turn into a butterfly. To their minds, that's perfectly logical. Gee! What a square school. Granted, they are on the right track. But this may not be the century to prove it.

Teachers often complain that the Aquarian child refuses to explain, step by step, how he arrived at his remarkable answer to a complicated maths problem before she finished writing it on the blackboard. There's a good, sensible reason. His Uranian intuition, that works by some kind of unseen radio waves, forced his mind through those steps so quickly, he just can't remember. Almost all Aquarian children were behind the delivery-room door when memory was passed out. Forgetting their address is frequent, forgetting their last name is uncomfortably possible, and forgetting what time to come home is par-for-the-course. Your brilliant – and he most likely is – Uranus youngster must be taught that his aim should encompass more than being a human computer. He needs to learn the importance of organizing his thoughts in logical order. Otherwise, a potential genius, philosopher, engineer, scientist, doctor, lawyer – gardener or cab driver (the last two if you're lucky) – can turn into an eccentric adult, headed in several directions at once, and end up going around in interesting, but not very profitable, circles.

Encourage him to participate in physical activity or a harmful inertia can take over, and he'll daydream the hours away. It often takes an emergency to spur Aquarian children to physical action, though they can have a great love for sports. Mentally, they're speed demons. But the body may be a bit slower, at least around the house. They may have an empathy for birds, trees, nature and the seashore. They'll always prefer their own, independent discovery to organized activity. You'll have to watch for a tendency to say 'I can't' to rationalize the urge to avoid responsibility. The Aquarian child may take the path of least resistance, if you let him. Teach him that he's only fooling himself. Let him make his own decisions, but encourage him to act on them.

Unspoken tension can deeply disturb him. These youngsters can almost see into the souls of others, and hear thoughts which haven't even been audibly expressed, which can disturb them and leave lasting feelings of unhappiness. Better encourage tranquillity and harmony, concentration, and memory, if you don't want an eccentric, nervous, absent-minded bachelor or spinster with unfulfilled dreams on your hands in thirty years or so.

Be careful what you say and how you say it with Aquarian youngsters. Suggestions planted in these fertile, remarkably acute Uranian minds in childhood, can take firm root and form fixed adult opinions. Undue emphasis on clean hands, repeated warnings, 'Don't drink out of my glass, it's dirty,' can cause the Aquarian youngster to grow up with exaggerated fears and carry his own goblet in his pocket when he goes visiting. Being so accident prone, you can imagine what will happen if he sits down suddenly with that goblet there. And he does do almost everything suddenly.

Aquarian boys and girls have multitudes of friends. They make at least ten new ones per day, from the street cleaner to the truant officer and the ex-parachutist who runs the sweet shop. He might even bring home a little friend named Rockefeller for lunch some day, too, but don't let it shake you. You're not raising a social snob. He won't know him from the dog catcher. He's just another 'pal'.

Adolescent problems of romance may never bother you. In fact, the Aquarian child may have to be reminded which sex is which. Few of these youngsters are boy crazy or girl crazy. Just plain crazy is more of a possibility, especially when they start wearing those weird clothes and parting their hair in such an odd way. This may be about the time his hidden love of poetry emerges, which should be encouraged. Your little Uranian has frogs in his pockets and stars in his eyes, but he's very special. He's a humanitarian. He loves people. Do you know how rare that is? As society moves into the Aquarian age, his unprejudiced wisdom is leading us. Aquarian boys and girls have been chosen by destiny to fulfil the promises of tomorrow – frogs and stars, pickle sandwiches and all. Just nickname him the 'Twentieth-Century Wonder', and let the neighbours guess why.

The Aquarius Boss

'What sort of things do you remember best?'
Alice ventured to ask.
'Oh, things that happened
the week after next.'

First of all, check again. Are you sure his birthday is late January or early February? Are you absolutely positive your boss is an Aquarian? Uranus-ruled executives are as rare as albino pandas. If you have one for a boss, you can't very well sell him to a zoo, but consider him a collector's item, anyway. Some day, he may be extremely valuable.

Seriously, the typical Aquarian would just about prefer starvation to the usual nine-to-five office routine. Most Aquarians dislike making decisions, they are uncomfortable giving orders, they have no particular desire to direct others and they're totally incompatible with stuffy board meetings, let alone stuffy vice-presidents. This doesn't mean Aquarians are not competent bosses. Uranus is full of surprises, and the totally unqualified Aquarian boss who turns out to be absolutely indispensable is one of them.

When an occasional Aquarian wanders into an executive position, burdened by all the above negative qualifications, he simply pulls a couple of new tricks out of his bag. He may be absent-minded and forgetful, eccentric and unpredictable, by turns shy and then bold, but he also has a mind like a bear trap hidden behind those strange, vague eyes and that detached, distant attitude. Add to that a highly tuned, perceptive intuitiveness, which makes you think he has a crystal ball tucked in a pocket. Throw in his uncanny ability to analyse, dissect and weigh the facts with insight as keen as a razor blade – and for good measure – his sure instinct in making a warm friend of everyone from the office boy to the firm's biggest customer. Back it up with the broad, liberal Uranus philosophy which sees miles into tomorrow, and catches the big picture in all its scope while others are floundering over details – and you see what I mean by surprises. Unfitted as the average Aquarian is for an executive role, he tosses off the job as casually as if he had been born to it, which he definitely was not.

There's the other side of the coin, too. He may possibly refer to you as 'My secretary, Miss . . . ah . . . ah . . . Miss . . . uh . . . what was your name again?' He can be maddening when he plans complicated programmes behind your back and springs them on you at the last minute. And I'm sure you've chafed under his frustrating habit of giving you a completely new and unexpected job to do, blithely neglecting to explain the reason behind the change. But confess now, under it all he really is rather a lovable old dear, isn't he? Most Aquarians are, once you get used to their peculiar ways, sudden changes and unexpected surprises. Also, I might add, their fixed opinions when they've made up their mind.

If I were you, I wouldn't try to borrow money from an Aquarian boss. If he's a typical Aquarian, he doesn't approve of people living beyond their income. Some Aquarians, of course, live in comfortable luxurious surroundings – but most of them are quite capable of living in one shabby room, while they spend twenty hours a

day promoting better housing for the poor. He won't be
impulsive about giving pay rises, but then, he won't be
stingy either. You'll get just about what you deserve with
your Aquarian boss. No more and no less. He can be
most generous when he thinks someone has done a top
job beyond the call of duty. Make no mistake. He'll expect
your best – your very best. Anything less brings the
danger of being politely and kindly, but firmly dropped.
Kerplunk – like that. An Aquarian has no use for people
who goof off or give half a day's work for a full day's
pay. To him, that's a form of dishonesty, and he hates
dishonesty in approximately the same degree that a cat
hates the water.

When it comes to your personal life, the Aquarian boss
hasn't the slightest desire either to judge you or advise
you. He does have a desire to know about it, however,
and you may find it hard to escape that probing Uranus
curiosity when it comes to your private affairs. But you
can tell him anything at all without worrying that he'll
be shocked. Nothing shocks him. He's the best student of
human nature in the zodiac, and he'll never look down
on you (any more than he'll look up to you). Both your
vices and your virtues blend into an interesting and
colourful pattern, as far as he's concerned. He takes it all
in his stride, and it doesn't make a ripple in his opinion
of you. The town drunk and the silly, giggling teenager are
as much his friends and as close to him as the president of
the local university and the state senator. You'll find literally no prejudice or discrimination if he's a true Aquarian.
In other words, you're in danger of being fired if he
catches you stealing stamps or hiding an unfinished report
in your desk – but if he discovers you're a bigamist, that
your father served two terms in prison, your son smokes

pot or your wife practises yoga on the back porch in her birthday suit, he'll just shrug, figure it's your life and probably defend you to your critics. The Aquarian boss won't be bothered one whit if you're a conservative politically and you paste a picture of Calvin Coolidge next to his painting of Franklin Roosevelt. He won't bat an eye at the news that you had to be poured into a taxi after the last office party. Just don't cheat him, lie to him or – heaven forbid – break your word to him. Promises and ethics and such are where he falls into the narrow-minded category.

Unlike the Aries or Leo boss, he won't exert energy trying to convince you that you're making a mistake in voting for that man, dating that girl or wearing that colour tie. And, unlike the Cancer, Capricorn or Libra boss, he won't hint and use persuasive strategy to change your viewpoint. Live your life the way you choose and more power to you for being an individualist is his creed. On the other hand, don't ever attempt to dictate his personal code to him, either. He won't show any anger, or probably even feel any. He may even smile and nod thoughtfully, with that faraway look in his eyes, but you might as well talk to the wall. He'll listen to almost anybody. Listen. That's all.

Although he forms his own code of ethics and keeps his own counsel in relation to his personal and private life, business decisions are another matter. He's very likely, if he's like the average Uranian man, to request everyone's opinion on projected procedures – and sometimes even ask a subordinate to make the final decision. There's a method to this madness, and it's not the same as with the indecisive Libran. Aquarius isn't passing the buck. He enjoys sitting back with an I-told-you-so look when the

decision you made (against his acutely accurate intuition)
falls as flat as a pancake – to teach you a lesson. You do
have to watch that. Aquarian bosses are usually willing
to give you all the rope you need to hang yourself with
and another several yards besides, if you ask for it. You're
lucky if he explains even once just exactly why he thinks
you're on the wrong track. When he's done that – which
is unusual enough – he won't explain a second time. You
take it from there. Catch it clearly the first time or you'll
get some confusing double-talk to remind you to pay
attention to what he says.

He expects you to be able to wiggle your antennae and
pick up anything you've missed out of the atmosphere.
He doesn't realize that other people don't have his
Uranian gift for absorbing information from three people
talking all at once, while he peels an orange, dials a phone
number and shuffles through a stack of inter-office memos.

Don't get too set in your ways around an Aquarian
executive. You're liable to walk in some morning and find
your office has been moved to another floor and he forgot
to tell you. There's always change in the air around this
man. You may have the unsettling experience of having
him sweep down unexpectedly one day with a big, warm,
friendly grin and throw your entire system out the window
– the system the office has been using since the Civil War.
In its place he'll substitute a new method, faster and less
cluttered with detail. You say you can't adjust that
quickly? You need at least six months to make the change
and the new system is Greek to you at this point? He
can't understand that. It's perfectly clear to him. Don't
worry, you'll catch on. He'll wait. He's patient.

And that he is. The normal Uranus-ruled mind may
be full of nervous curiosity just beneath the surface, but

generally the Aquarian takes it fairly easy, and projects an image of calm and thoughtful deliberation. You'll notice I said generally. Of course, there was the time he actually ran out of the office to catch those six fire engines, the turtle race he staged on his carpet with real turtles, and the day he had those miniature TV sets delivered to each desk during the World Series. And of course there was that morning he took over the switchboard, just to see what it was like, mixed up all the calls, disconnected everyone, accidentally got a big TV network VIP on a crossed wire and sold him a half-a-million-dollar deal – then forgot the man's name when he came in to sign the contract. But normally he's placid and controlled. So he's a little eccentric now and then: he has the water cooler moved once a month so you can't find it, and he likes to change your day off with no notice. What are a few minor annoyances like that when you work for a boss who's sincerely fascinated by that book you're writing on Kansas City jazz? And how can you stay mad at a boss who doesn't mind if the bookkeeper grows a beard, his secretary wears white fur boots with rhinestone heels to work or the new filing clerk parks his bicycle in the reception room?

He may spend one day talking your ears off, and the next week secluded inside his office, ignoring staff, customers and suppliers, deep in lonely thought. He's resting his soul, and those periods of retreat are necessary. Regardless of how recently you joined the firm, he'll consider you his friend. He's even good friends with the competition. No matter what it says on your company letterhead, the real business of your Aquarian boss is friendship. Somebody discussing today's corporate conformity recently said, 'Give me back the good, old-time

individualist executive with the gravy spots on his tie,
who got things done without calling a committee meeting
for every little snag.' The poor man was undoubtedly
undergoing a rush of nostalgia for an Aquarian boss he
had years ago.

Those of you who work for a Uranian probably don't
have the common problem of the boss's wife dropping in
unexpectedly while things are a mess and the painters are
tearing the reception room apart. She's lucky if she knows
where he works, let alone has permission to drop in on
him. Aquarians don't confide every little activity to their
wives. I used to live next door to the February-born executive of a research firm, who once didn't get around to
telling his wife he had to fly to Europe on business until
he arrived there and noticed he didn't have any clean
shirts. (He was quite put out about it, and he told her so
when he phoned her from Paris. Somehow, it was all her
fault. She should have anticipated he might make a trip.)

Funny how you kept remembering all the idiosyncrasies
of your own Aquarian executive last week while you
watched him get the *Man of the Year* award from the mayor
at that big formal banquet. You had just decided that,
regardless of his unpredictable ways and his dippy habits,
he was actually one of the most distinguished bosses a
person could have. Then you happened to look down
under the table – and there were his feet tapping the rug
impatiently, clad in neat black dress shoes, wearing one
blue sock and one yellow sock.

The Aquarius Employee

Twinkle, twinkle, little bat!
How I wonder what you're at!
Up above the world you fly,
Like a tea-tray in the sky.

You shouldn't have any trouble spotting your Aquarian
employee. He's the one with all the friends. You know,
the one who forgot his brief case this morning – the same
man who casually dropped in your office last month to
borrow your fountain pen and left behind a production
idea which has saved your company $30,000 in overtime
so far, according to the latest check by the auditor.

It should also be a cinch to remember the day you
hired him. He's that fellow you thought came in to sell
you a box at Yankee Stadium – then you decided he
was soliciting funds for Shakespeare-in-the-Park, finally
figured he was taking one of those political polls – and
didn't realize until after he left that he had actually
stopped by to apply for a job. If you don't remember him,
it's five-to-one your secretary does. Aquarius men seem
to make an instant and lasting impression on women,
even those who look like neglected, underfed puppy dogs
with figures loosely resembling Ichabod Crane's. Some
people might jump to the hasty conclusion this is the
mother-instinct, but they would be wrong. The real
Uranus attraction for females is the Aquarian's absolute
indifference to their existence. It drives them to distrac-
tion. He's a challenge they can't resist – so they either

retaliate by trying to vamp him or by snubbing him back, neither of which makes the slightest impression on your Aquarian employee. He can be totally blind to a female co-worker for weeks, literally not seeing her, then one fine spring morning suddenly startle her with the information that her eyes are the exact shade of a robin's egg he once found in a tree, and she's gone. I mean, completely lost. She may not type a word for the rest of the day.

Life with an Aquarian employee can be exhilarating and leave you a little breathless. It's not that they're extroverts or flamboyant or practical jokers. Quite the reverse. Many Aquarians are sober, cool, aloof and removed from the mad world around them. The only trouble is that they've removed themselves fifty years ahead, and when they rocket back to the present every few days or so, they've bagged some unusual ideas from the stratosphere. If you're a smart boss, you'll invite the Uranus man to your office for a chat once a week. It could be profitable. Who knows what you might pick up? When he tells you in the proper technical language exactly what's wrong with that loose screw under the fourth bolt in the new machine that keeps breaking down, you may start to wonder if he *has* been to Mars and back since you saw him on the elevator yesterday. Especially after you check personnel records and see that he didn't take a course in science or mechanics at college. Still, the informal conference with him may not always turn out so profitably. He may leave after that little confidential talk with your cheque for a few thousand dollars for the preservation of Basketball on Indian Reservations – or the Research Society for Investigating Psychic Phenomena in Smyrna. The Aquarian interests are world-wide.

Chances are this seemingly quiet, brilliant and friendly

young man won't stay around long enough for you to remember his face. The Aquarian male will either begin at the top, work his way up there in a few weeks, decide to go it alone as a composer, photographer, ornithologist, dancer, singer, clown, writer, juggler, athlete, geologist, radio or TV announcer, etc. – or leave you to drift from job to job 'looking for himself'. Some day he'll find himself, too. When he does, he usually stays in one place for a lifetime. Until that moment of truth, however, our Uranus-ruled friends spend a period of time just roaming around, experimenting, learning, looking, investigating, and picking up new friends.

He's not sentimental by nature. He has a scientific attitude, but there's also a strong interest in people, what makes them laugh and what makes them cry. An Aquarian does not lean towards emotionalism (except rarely when he's in the clutch of an eccentric rush of behaviour, perhaps a reaction to some very disturbing personal experience). Unfortunately, his ideas and opinions are often considered irrational and impractical, but that's just because his critics aren't tuned to his frequency – half a century ahead. Imagine how your grandmother felt when some Aquarian back in the nineties tried to describe colour television and astronauts landing on the moon. That gives you a fair idea of the reception Uranus-ruled people get today when they start in on their theory of a time machine, and how it could be designed with safety valves so a defective switch won't get you lost somewhere in 1770.

You may notice the Aquarian employee with a different friend each week or so. It's difficult for him to be satisfied with any one individual at a time, since his sympathies

run into so many channels. It's common for him, therefore, to give more friendship than he receives.

The first thing you may have to do is decide which kind
of Aquarian you have employed. There's only one basic
Uranus type – but there are two ways in which the Aquarian nature can manifest itself. The first kind is the suave,
pipe-smoking, professor type, with a relaxed manner and
not a few eccentric habits, who lives in an elegant, but
curious apartment full of Egyptian mummies, a tree from
India planted in the centre of the room, bells from Suma-
tra, sixteenth-century tables and early American rockets,
plus a mod painting or two and maybe an old aeroplane
propeller hanging over the fireplace. He dines on gourmet
foods like roasted grasshoppers and steak tartare with
ant's eggs sprinkled on top. He's usually brilliant.

The other kind lives in a tiny room over the subway,
eats mustard sandwiches and watches his favourite TV
show on the first set ever manufactured. He scatters his
inventions all over the corner table, picks out tunes on a
dusty piano, and washes the dishes once a week. He is
also brilliant. The trouble is, when you get them both out
in normal society, it's hard to tell the difference.

Both are conscientious workers. Both have a high
degree of intelligence, as well as uncanny perception and
a fine sensitivity to everyone around them. They each
soak up knowledge while appearing to be engrossed in
some abstract theory. Their memories are weak but their
intuitive powers more than make up for it. They're
extremely odd in their habits, kind and sympathetic, usually very courteous, and they wear unusual combinations
of clothing. They're each loyal, honest and have a strict
code which is never violated. Both are bachelors and they
number about five thousand good friends each, ranging

from Leonard Bernstein and Joe Namath to Scarface Al and Minnie, the apple lady, who takes numbers. So you see? An Aquarian is an Aquarian. A pipe, a mustard sandwich or a couple of Egyptian mummies between a couple of lotus trees have nothing at all to do with it.

You can be safe in assuming your Aquarian worker is giving you a full day's work for his pay. Although he's probably the real cause of your secretary's severe skin rash her doctor can't diagnose or cure, he may end up on the front page of *The New York Times* some day, being presented with a plaque or something and you can say 'I knew him when'. He can also contribute some pretty sane, concrete thinking to your firm which will possibly even result in bringing it up to the Twentieth Century. He's utterly trustworthy with company secrets, and probably the best customer's man you can find, because he'll make friends with your coldest client and wonder why everyone thought he was so tough to deal with. To the Aquarian, he's just another human with some intriguing aspect to his personality to be uncovered with a few polite, direct questions and a little observation.

This employee isn't likely to nudge you constantly for a pay rise, because money is usually down there on the bottom of his list, along with women. But he's shrewd enough to know his worth, and it wouldn't be wise to take advantage of him. He may cause some raised eyebrows, but he'll seldom cause any scandal or petty office gossip. You won't find him filled with much intense, driving ambition, yet he has one of the finest minds in the zodiac. If you should decide he knows enough to make him your partner, he'll never steal the business from you – and he can be a most decided asset, possibly even bring world-wide prestige to the firm some day.

When he does eventually decide to get married, you may lose a good secretary (he won't want his wife to work), but you want the poor girl's skin rash to clear up, don't you?

Afterword

How many miles to Babylon?
Three-score-miles-and-ten.
Can I get there by candlelight?
Yes – and back again!
Mother Goose

Shake her snow-white feathers, tune in to her nonsensical wavelength, and old Mother Goose may show us a secret message. There may be a pearl of wisdom hidden in the apparently childish prattle of her nursery rhyme.

How many miles to Babylon? It seems to be quite a leap from the sandal-clad people of Chaldea and the jewelled, perfumed Pharaohs of Egypt to the space age – from the lost continent of Atlantis to the jet-propelled Twentieth Century. But how far is it, really? Perhaps only a dream or two.

Alone among the sciences, astrology has spanned the centuries and made the journey intact. We shouldn't be surprised that it remains with us, unchanged by time – because astrology is truth – and truth is eternal. Echoing the men and women of the earliest known civilizations, today's moderns repeat identical phrases: 'Is Venus your ruling planet?' 'I was born when the Sun was in Taurus.' 'Is your Mercury in Gemini too?' 'Wouldn't you just know he's an Aquarian?'

Astrological language is a golden cord that binds us to a dim past while it prepares us for an exciting future of planetary explorations. Breath-taking Buck Rogers ad-

vances in all fields of science are reminding us that 'there
are more things in heaven and earth, Horatio, than are
dreamt of in your philosophy' (even if your name is Sam
or Fanny instead of Horatio). Dick Tracy's two-way wrist
radio is no longer a fantastic dream – it's reality – and
Moon Maid's powerful weapon has been matched by the
miracle of the laser beam, the highly concentrated light
that makes lead run like water and penetrates the hardest
substances known to man. Jules Verne and Flash Gordon
are now considered pretty groovy prophets, so there were
obviously important secrets buried in those way-out
adventures twenty thousand leagues under the sea and
many trillions of leagues above the earth.

Could it be that the science-fiction writers and cartoon-
ists have a better idea of the true distance between yesterday, today and tomorrow than the white-coated men in
their sterile, chrome laboratories? Einstein knew that time
was only relative. The poets have always been aware –
and the wise men, down through the ages. The message
is not new. Long before today's overwhelming interest
in astrology, daring men of vision like Plato, Ptolemy,
Hippocrates and Columbus respected its wisdom; and
they've been kept good company by the likes of Galileo,
Ben Franklin, Thomas Jefferson, Sir Isaac Newton and
Dr Carl Jung. You can add President John Quincy Adams
to the list; also great astronomers like Tycho Brahe,
Johannes Kepler and Dr Gustave Stromberg. And don't
forget RCA's brilliant research scientist, John Nelson,
famed mathematician, Dr Kuno Foelsch and Pulitzer
prize winner, John O'Neill. None of these men were high
school drop-outs.

In 1953, Dr Frank A. Brown, Jr, of North-western University, made a startling discovery while he was experi-

menting with some oysters. Science has always assumed that oysters open and close with the cycle of the tides of their birthplace. But when Dr Brown's oysters were taken from the waters of Long Island Sound and placed in a tank of water in his Evanston, Illinois laboratory, a strange pattern emerged.

Their new home was kept at an even temperature, and the room was illuminated with a steady, dim light. For two weeks, the displaced oysters opened and closed their shells with the same rhythm as the tides of Long Island Sound – one thousand miles away. Then they suddenly snapped shut, and remained that way for several hours. Just as Dr Brown and his research team were about to consider the case of the homesick oysters closed, an odd thing happened. The shells opened wide once again. Exactly four hours after the high tide at Long Island Sound – at the precise moment when there would have been a high tide at Evanston, Illinois, if it were on the sea coast – a new cycle began. They were adapting their rhythm to the new geographical latitude and longitude. By what force? By the moon, of course. Dr Brown had to conclude that the oysters' energy cycles are ruled by the mysterious lunar signal that controls the tides.

Human energy and emotional cycles are governed by the same kind of planetary forces, in a much more complicated network of magnetic impulses from all the planets. Science recognizes the moon's power to move great bodies of water. Since man himself consists of seventy per cent water, why should he be immune to such forceful planetary pulls? The tremendous effects of magnetic gravity on orbiting astronauts as they get closer to the planets is well known. What about the proven correlation between lunar motion and women's cycles, including childbirth – and the repeated testimony of doctors and nurses in the wards of mental hospitals, who are only too familiar with the influence of the moon's changes on their patients? Did you ever talk to a policeman who had to work a rough beat on the night of a full moon? Try to find a farmer who will sink a fence rail, slaughter a pig or plant crops without astrological advice from his trusted *Farmer's Almanac*. The movements of the moon and the planets are as important to him as the latest farm bill controversy in Congress.

Of all the heavenly bodies, the Moon's power is more visible and dramatic, simply because it's the closest body to the earth. But the Sun, Venus, Mars, Mercury, Jupiter, Saturn, Uranus, Neptune and Pluto exercise their influences just as surely, even though from farther away. Scientists are aware that plants and animals are influenced by cycles at regular intervals, and that the cycles are governed through forces such as electricity in the air, fluctuations in barometric pressure and the gravitational field. These earthly forces are originally triggered by magnetic vibrations from outer space, where the planets live, and from where they send forth their unseen waves. Phases of the moon, showers of gamma rays, cosmic rays, X-rays, undulations of the pear-shaped electromagnetic field and other influences from extraterrestrial sources are constantly penetrating and bombarding the atmosphere around us. No living organism escapes it, nor do the minerals. Nor do we.

Dr Harold S. Burr, emeritus Professor of Anatomy at Yale's Medical School, states that a complex magnetic field not only establishes the pattern of the human brain at birth, but continues to regulate and control it through life. He further states that the human central nervous system is a superb receptor of electromagnetic energies, the finest in nature. (We may walk with a fancier step, but we hear the same drummer as the oysters.) The ten million cells in our brains form a myriad of possible circuits through which electricity can channel.

Therefore, the mineral and chemical content and the electrical cells of our bodies and brains respond to the magnetic influence of every sunspot, eclipse and planetary movement. We are synchronized, like all other living organisms, metals and minerals, to the ceaseless ebb and flow of the universe; but we need not be imprisoned by it, because of our own free will. The soul, in other words, is superior to the power of the planets. Yet unfortunately, most of us fail to use our free will (i.e. the power of the soul), and are just about as helpless to control our destinies as Lake Michigan or an ear of corn. The purpose of the astrologer is to help us gain the knowledge of how to avoid drifting downstream – how to fight the current.

Astrology is an art as well as a science. Though lots of people would like to ignore that basic fact, it can't be overlooked. There are astrologers who tremble with anger at the mere mention of intuition in relation to astrology. They send out fiery blasts against any hint of such a correlation, and frantically insist that 'Astrology is an exact science, based on mathematics. It should never be mentioned in the same breath with intuitive powers.' I regard their opinions as sincere, but logic forces me to ask why these must be so totally separate. Should they be? Even the layman today is attempting, through books, games and parlour or laboratory testing, to determine his or her ESP potential. Why not astrologers? Are they supposed to bury their heads in the sand like ostriches concerning the development of a sixth sense, or the existence of it in some individuals?

Granted, the calculation of an astrological chart, based on mathematical data and astronomical facts, is an exact science. But medicine is also science, based on fact and research. Yet, all good doctors admit that medicine is an art as well. The intuitive diagnostician is recognized by his colleagues. Physicians will tell you that they each have, in varying degrees, a certain sensitivity, which is an invaluable aid in interpreting the provable facts of medicine. To synthesize medical theories, to interpret the results of laboratory tests in relation to the patient's individual history, is never cut and dried. It simply couldn't be done without intuitive perception on the part of the doctor. Otherwise, medicine could simply be computerized.

Music is also scientifically based – on the inflexible law of mathematics – as everyone who has ever studied chord progressions knows. Musical interludes are governed by ratios of whole numbers – a science, indisputably – it's also an art. Anyone can be taught to play *Clair de lune* or *The Warsaw Concerto* correctly but it's the sensitivity or intuitive perception of a Van Cliburn that separates him from the rest of us. The notes and chords are always the same, mathematically exact. The interpretation, however, is different – an obvious reality which has nothing to do with present definitions of the word science.

Many intelligent people can study or teach astrology successfully, even brilliantly, but few are able to add the dimension of sensitive interpretation or intuitive perception that makes the science of astrology ultimately satisfying as an art. Of course, one doesn't have to be a psychic or a medium to give an accurate and helpful astrological analysis, yet any intuition on the part of the astrologer is clearly an asset to his synthesis of the natal chart. Naturally, the intuitive astrologer must also be well versed in mathematical calculation and must strictly observe the scientific fundamentals of his art. Assuming he is and does, he's using a powerful combination of both conscious and subconscious abilities, so you needn't be frightened into avoiding competent professionals who are able to make both an art and a science of their work. If anything, you'll be lucky to find one. Sensitive perception is rare in any field.

The popularity of astrology today is bringing all the quacks out of the woodwork, and there aren't as many qualified astrologers and teachers as there should be. Possibly within the next decade, astrologers will be recognized professionals, who have graduated from an 'astral science' course in a leading college. The important study of the influence of the planets on human behaviour will be then taught in the modern halls of ivy, as it was once taught in the great universities of Europe. Students will be accepted only if their natal charts reveal an ability to teach or research in astrology or to give a personal analysis; and the courses will be as tough as those in any law or medical school. The subjects of magnetic weather conditions, biology, chemistry, geology, astronomy, higher mathematics, sociology, comparative religions, philosophy and psychology will be required – as well as instruction in calculating an astrological chart and interpreting it – and graduates will proudly set up a plaque reading: 'John Smith – Astrologer, DAS' (Doctor of Astral Science).

At the present stage of research and acceptance, the safest and sanest approach to astrology by the layman is to become thoroughly acquainted with the twelve signs,

which is on a par with becoming acquainted with the
theories of medicine by studying first aid or sensible health
rules.

Mankind will some day discover that astrology, medicine, religion, astronomy and psychiatry are all one. When
they are blended, each will be whole. Until then, each
will be slightly defective.

There is an area of confusion in astrology about which
opinions clash. Reincarnation. There's not a person today
who doesn't have either a positive or negative approach
to the law of karma. You can't avoid learning and reading
about it any more than you can avoid exposure to the
ouija board under the Uranus influence of this Twentieth-
Century movement into the Aquarian age.

Esoteric astrologers believe, as I do, that astrology is
incomplete unless properly interpreted with the law of
karma as its foundation. There are others who emphatically deny this, especially in the western world, to which
astrology is comparatively new. You needn't accept
reincarnation to derive benefit from astrology; and the
proof of the soul's existence in previous lives, however
logical, has never been scientifically established (though
some mighty convincing circumstantial evidence is available, including documented cases and the Bible itself).
Because of its very nature, reincarnation may for ever
elude absolute, tangible proof. The ancients taught that
the evolved soul must reach the point of seeking the truth
of karma, in order to end the cycle of re-birth. Therefore,
faith in reincarnation is a gift – a reward for the soul
advanced enough to search for the meaning of its existence
in the universe and its karmic obligations in the present
life. Proof of this deep mystery would remove the individual free will of discovery, so perhaps man must always

look for the answers to reincarnation in his own heart. But he should do so only after intelligent study of what other minds have found to be both false and true. Books written about the amazing prophet Edgar Cayce, will give the curious layman a better understanding of what it's all about, and there are many other excellent works on the market concerning reincarnation, which will help you establish for yourself whether the subject is worthy of your consideration or just so much black magic. That's the only way to approach such a personal matter as life and death – by yourself – after a thorough examination of the pros and cons.

We are heading in the direction of new respect for unseen influences, and the current interest in mental telepathy is a good example. Huge sums of money have been and are being spent by NASA in ESP tests with selected astronauts to determine the possibility of transferring mental messages through sense perception, as an emergency measure against a breakdown of present communications between earth and astronaut. Russia is rumoured to be far ahead of us in this area of research, another reason why dogmatic, materialistic thinking must go.

The excitement of distinguished scientists about experiments with these invisible wavelengths between human minds has gained the attention of the medical doctors. Medicine has long admitted that such ailments as ulcers and strep throat are brought on by mental strain, or emotional tension, and now physicians are advancing serious theories that there is a definite relationship between the personality of the patient and the growth and development of cancer. Recent articles by well-known doctors have urged the co-operation of psychiatrists in determining in advance which patient may be susceptible, so the disease can be treated early or even prevented. Yet astrology has always known that disease is triggered by the mind and emotions, and can be controlled or eliminated the same way; also that people born under certain planetary influences are either susceptible or immune to particular diseases and accidents. The knowledge medicine seeks is in the patient's carefully calculated, detailed natal chart, clearly shown by his planetary positions and aspects at birth.

The astrologer–physicians in ancient Egypt practised brain surgery with refined techniques, a fact recently proven by archaeological and anthropological discoveries. Today's progressive doctors are quietly checking the astrological sign the moon is transiting before surgery, imitating the Greek physicians of centuries ago, who followed Hippocrates' precept of: 'Touch not with metal that part of the anatomy ruled by the sign the Moon is transiting, or to which the transiting Moon is in square or opposition by aspect.' There's much that's compelling and important to say about medical astrology and its value to the physician in the cause and prevention of illness, but it's such a huge subject, it must wait for another volume.

Moving from medicine to travel, several insurance companies and airlines are secretly investigating the possible relationship between fatal plane crashes and the natal charts of the passengers and crew. So time marches on – from ancient knowledge of planetary influences – retrograding back to materialistic thinking – and forward again to truth. Down through the centuries the planets remain unchanged in their grandeur and their orbs. The stars which shone over Babylon and the stable in Bethlehem still shine as brightly over the Empire State Building and your front garden today. They perform their cycles with the same mathematical precision, and they will continue to affect each thing on earth, including man, as long as the earth exists.

Always remember that astrology is not fatalistic. The stars incline, they do not compel. Most of us are carried along in blind obedience to the influence of the planets and our electromagnetic birth patterns, as well as to our environment, our heredity and the wills of those stronger than us. We show no perception, therefore no resistance; and our horoscopes fit us like a fingerprint. We're moved like pawns on a chess board in the game of life, even while some of us scoff at or ignore the very powers which are moving us. But anyone can rise above the afflictions of his nativity. By using free will, or the powers of the soul, anyone can dominate his moods, change his character, control his environment and the attitudes of those close to him. When we do this, we become movers in the chess game, instead of the pawns.

Do you refrain from following your star by saying, 'I just wasn't born with the strength or the ability?' You were born with more of each than Helen Keller, who called on the deep, inner power of her will to overcome being blind, deaf and dumb. She replaced these natal afflictions with fame, wealth, respect and the love of thousands, and she conquered her planetary influences.

Do constant fears keep you from seeing tomorrow? Do melancholy and pessimism colour your rainbows grey before you even reach out to touch them? Actress Patricia Neal substituted iron nerve for gloomy apprehension. She smiled at tragedy, and her grin gave her enough emotional energy to astound her doctors by literally forcing the paralysis of a near-fatal stroke to vaporize.

Do newspaper headlines have you convinced America is doomed to oblivion in the near future, through the stalemate of hot and cold wars, lack of national and international understanding, rising crime rates, injustice, prejudice, moral decadence, loss of ethics and the possibility of nuclear destruction? Winston Churchill once faced certain defeat for himself personally – and for his country. But he put a twinkle in his eyes, a piece of steel in his spine and a prayer in his heart. That triple combination wrought a miracle, as the courage of one man aroused thousands to blind optimism and stubborn strength. The resulting magnetic vibrations melted the lead of fear, inspired the world and made victory the prize. He refused to be a pawn of the planets or let his country be the pawn of their influence.

You say such people are special? But these could be your miracles. All of them. There's enough magnetic power in you to make you immune to the strongest planetary pulls, now or in the future. What a pity to submit so easily and let your potential remain unrealized.

When both hate and fear are conquered, the will is then free and capable of immense power. This is the message of your own nativity, hidden in the silent stars. Listen to it.

An ancient legend tells of a man who went to a wise mystic to ask for the key to power and occult secrets. He was taken to the edge of a clear lake, and told to kneel down. Then the wise one disappeared, and the man was left alone, staring down at his own reflected image in the water.

'What I do, you can do also.' 'Ask, and you shall receive.' 'Knock, and it shall be opened unto you.' 'Seek the truth, and the truth shall set you free.'

'How many miles to Babylon? Three-score-miles-and-ten. Can I get there by candlelight? Yes – and back again.' Is it a poem, or is it a riddle? Each thing in the universe is part of the universal law, and astrology is the basis of that law. Out of astrology grew religion, medicine and astronomy, not the other way round.

There's a sculptured zodiac in the temple of Thebes, so old that its origin has never been determined. Atlantis? Perhaps. But wherever it's from and whoever carved its symbols, its message is eternal: you are endless galaxies – and you have seen but one star.